Columbia University

Contributions to Education

Teachers College Series

No. 412

AMS PRESS
NEW YORK

TRENDS IN EDUCATIONAL OCCUPATIONS

AN EXAMINATION OF THE WAXING AND WANING OCCUPA-
TIONS IN THE PUBLIC SCHOOL SYSTEMS OF CERTAIN
CITIES IN THE UNITED STATES FROM 1898 TO 1928

144164

BY

MARJORIE RANKIN, Ph.D.

TEACHERS COLLEGE, COLUMBIA UNIVERSITY
CONTRIBUTIONS TO EDUCATION, No. 412

BUREAU OF PUBLICATIONS
Teachers College, Columbia University
NEW YORK CITY
1930

Library of Congress Cataloging in Publication Data

Rankin, Marjorie, 1888-
   Trends in educational occupations.

   Reprint of the 1930 ed., issued in series: Teachers
College, Columbia University. Contributions to
education, no. 412.
   Originally presented as the author's thesis, Columbia.
   Bibliography: p.
   1. Educators—United States—Statisitcs.
2. Teachers—Supply and demand—United States.
I. Title. II. Series: Columbia University. Teachers
College. Contributions to education, no. 412.
LB1775.R26   1972   331.7'61'370973   74-177179
ISBN 0-404-55412-1

Reprinted by Special Arrangement with Teachers
College Press, New York, New York

From the edition of 1930, New York
First AMS edition published in 1972
Manufactured in the United States

AMS PRESS, INC.
NEW YORK, N. Y.   10003

ACKNOWLEDGMENTS

The writer wishes to express her sincere appreciation to Dr. Harry D. Kitson, of Teachers College, Columbia University. He suggested the problem, was chairman of her dissertation committee, and constantly encouraged and assisted in the undertaking. Dr. Kitson is largely responsible for whatever may be of value in the results.

Thanks are also due to Dr. W. S. Elsbree, Dr. Harold Clark, and Dr. Clarence Linton, of Teachers College, Columbia University for their helpful criticism and careful reading of the manuscript. Grateful acknowledgment is made to Miss Esther Derring of the Library of Teachers College for her cheerful and ever-ready help in looking up and suggesting references.

Special mention should be made of those in the different cities visited who so kindly gave the writer access to their records and helped her to examine the many pages of board minutes for desired data.

M. R.

CONTENTS

TRENDS IN EDUCATIONAL OCCUPATIONS

CHAPTER I

NEED FOR ANALYZING THE EDUCATIONAL OCCUPATIONS

IMPORTANCE OF EDUCATION AS AN OCCUPATION

In point of numbers involved, education is one of the most important occupations in the United States. The 1920 Census showed that among the forty-seven million wage-earners there were only four groups larger than the educational group: retail dealers, sales persons, servants, and clerks, each with over a million. At that time there were 761,766 persons engaged in education.

But numbers is not the chief criterion of importance. Probably all would agree that, from the point of view of the future of the country, the educators of the young stand very high in importance.

INFORMATION SHOULD BE AVAILABLE FOR PROSPECTIVE EDUCATORS

Persons who contemplate entering such an important occupation should know in advance what is involved in the occupation. They should know what and how many educational positions there are; what types of preparation they require; whether the usual method of entrance is from a training school or by promotion; the hours of work per day, months of work per year, and vacations; the earnings to be expected; the general level of ability required for success in each branch; and the relation between supply and demand in the field each year. They should know about pensions, age limits, life certificates, and other phases.

All this information and much more should be available to young people who are considering education as a career.

Although a considerable amount of information is being gathered, there is one important question which has never been answered: How many educational occupations are there and

1

what is the nature of them? During the past generation or two the field has been undergoing a stage of differentiation and numerous specialties have emerged. How many there are has never been ascertained. This investigation attempts to answer that question.

Another fundamental question concerns the distribution within the occupation. What is the numerical distribution of educators among these special fields? Which field employs the greatest number? What is the order of the other fields in point of numbers employed?

In order to estimate the future demands in each of these educational specialties we should know the rate at which they are multiplying. This calls for a historical investigation; and such investigation, covering the thirty years from 1898 to 1928, has been made in this study. It is hoped that the information here presented will fill a fundamental need in programs of vocational guidance for prospective educators.

CHAPTER II

MAKING A CENSUS OF THE EDUCATIONAL OCCUPATIONS

AIMS

As stated in Chapter I, the aims of the investigation were (1) to classify the educational tasks, (2) to find the present distribution of teachers among various special fields, and (3) to study the evolution of education, noting the trends during the past thirty years, with their probable implications for the future.

PLAN

It was at first intended to study the public school systems of all the large cities in the country for the year 1927-28 and as many of these as possible for the years 1897-98, 1907-08, and 1917-18. A preliminary survey, however, showed that the information desired was nowhere in print and that the public school systems did not have such data on record. This complication of the task prohibited the wide range of the plan as at first conceived, and it was therefore limited to certain large city systems. The justification for this procedure was that the largest cities would show distributions of teachers more nearly representative of the country as a whole than the same number of smaller cities. Four smaller cities were included in order to make sure that the distributions were fairly comparable. Altogether data were obtained concerning 78,713 teachers, representing a population area of 14,590,274—more than 10 per cent of the population of the United States.

SOURCES

When this survey was undertaken it was thought that the facts wanted would have been collected and printed in city or state minutes or in certain reports of the National Education Association and that the historical study could be made by compiling data from the old reports. As stated above, however,

3

careful search through city, state, and national reports showed that the facts sought in this investigation had not been printed nor even filed in permanent records. Original documents were therefore sought. Three sources yielded data: City directories, school board minutes, and pay rolls. Each of these contained the name and position of each worker in the school system. These were tallied off so that the resulting charts showed the number of persons in each administrative and supervisory position and the number teaching each subject. From these sources it was also possible to make a complete list of all educational positions as they actually existed, not as contemplated in a catalogue or prospectus, and to learn when each new position was introduced.

PROCEDURE

It was found that many teachers taught more than one subject. For tabulation purposes, if a teacher taught two subjects, she was considered as teaching half time in each subject, regardless of the actual number of hours in each; if she taught three subjects she was credited with one-third in each. This was done for two reasons: the directories gave no finer classification, and, considering the many thousand teachers being dealt with, a more refined classification did not seem necessary.

From the 1920 Census the twelve cities with a population of 500,000 or over were selected. Two of these cities, however, could not be included in the study because data were not available. Four smaller cities were chosen for study in order to see if they presented conditions comparable with those in the large cities. The cities studied are listed in Table 1.

In the case of four of the cities studied the investigator visited the office of the board of education and made the necessary tabulation directly from the pay rolls or minutes. In the case of the other cities a letter was sent to each superintendent of schools explaining the nature of the investigation and asking for the number of administrative and supervisory officers, the number of teachers in each grade of the elementary school, and the number of persons teaching each subject in the secondary schools; where this information had not been collected, a copy of the school directory was requested. Cordial replies were received from all the officials. The records came in tabulated

TABLE 1

LIST OF CITIES STUDIED, WITH DATE OF REPORT, AND THE TOTAL POPULATION
POPULATION OF EACH CITY AS GIVEN BY PATTERSON'S *American
Educational Directory*

CITY	DATE OF REPORT				POPULATION IN 1928
Baltimore	--	--	1917	1928	733,826
Los Angeles	1898	1907	1917	1928	1,300,328
Philadelphia	1897	1907	1918	1928	1,979,364
Pittsburgh	1898	1906-7	1918	1928-29	588,343
Providence	1897-98	1907-8	1917-18	1928-29	267,918
Warren, Pa.	1897-98	1907-8	1917-18	1928-29	14,272
Boston	--	--	--	1928	748,060
Buffalo	--	--	--	1929	538,016
Cleveland	--	--	--	1928	936,455
Newark	--	--	--	1928	452,513
New York	--	--	--	1928	5,621,151
San Francisco	--	--	--	1928	557,530
St. Louis	--	--	--	1928-29	821,583
Waltham, Mass.	--	--	--	1928	30,915
Total	--	--	--	--	14,590,274

NOTE: The dashes indicate that data were not obtained. The total population of the six cities for which data were available for the three decades prior to 1928 is 4,884,051.

TABLE 2

TOTAL NUMBER OF TEACHERS FOR EACH YEAR FOR EACH CITY STUDIED

CITY	NUMBER OF TEACHERS			
	1898	1908	1918	1928
Baltimore	--	--	2,294	3,161
Cleveland	--	--	3,529	5,041
Los Angeles	480	1,085	3,079	9,770
Philadelphia	3,287	4,294	6,272	9,033
Pittsburgh	920	1,263	2,711	3,449
Providence	605	744	999	1,487
Warren	39	56	91	125
Boston	--	--	--	4,575
Buffalo	--	--	--	3,625
Newark	--	--	--	2,106
New York	--	--	--	30,451
San Francisco	--	--	--	2,485
St. Louis	--	--	--	3,120
Waltham	--	--	--	285
Total	5,331	9,270	18,975	78,713

form from Cleveland and Baltimore for 1928. No records in the detailed form necessary for this study were available in Detroit and Chicago, and consequently these two cities had to be excluded. From the other cities school directories were received.

The number of cities for each section of the study varies from seven to fourteen. The total list of cities studied, with their population for 1928 as shown by Patterson's *American Educational Directory,* and the total number of teachers for each city for each of the years studied are given in Tables 1 and 2.

CHAPTER III

NAMING AND CLASSIFYING THE EDUCATIONAL OCCUPATIONS

The first step in this survey of educational occupations was to list them. This appeared at first to be very simple. The first classification comprised two groups: (1) Administration and Supervision and (2) Teaching Force. An attempt was made to list the titles found in the directories under these two heads, but many titles appeared which could not be so listed. For example, how should the following positions be classified: nurse, librarian, piano tuner, cafeteria manager, structural engineer, school psychologist? The result was that five groups, instead of the original two, were necessary: (1) Maintenance, (2) Personal Service, (3) Professional Service, (4) Administration and Supervision, and (5) Teaching Force. The names of the positions in each group are given in the lists on the following pages.

Even with five headings, classification of certain positions presented considerable difficulty. The investigator made a tentative listing, taking into consideration the different viewpoints. Through the courtesy of Professor W. S. Elsbree, one of the classes in educational administration in Teachers College, Columbia University, gave valuable assistance in the classifying. Later the investigator saw some changes which should have been made in classification, but after the tallying had been completed it was impossible to change the lists without destroying the validity of the original tables.

In studying the graphic presentation of the data as given in the charts in Chapter IV, it will be necessary for the reader to refer to the classification list in order to know exactly what is included in each. All positions which could not be classed as Maintenance, Administration, or Teaching were divided between Professional and Personal, according to whether or not they involved direct contact with the student body. The divisions were hard to make and, as stated above, were arbitrarily made

7

after much deliberation. These lists (Lists 1 to 5) are given alphabetically for the convenience of the reader.

The list of teachers contains much overlapping and probably some of the titles cover the same work in different school systems. The inclusion of two such titles, however, indicates that in some schools they stood for different duties.

The division of Maintenance was left out, since accurate figures from all the systems were not available. Percentages were obtained for the other main divisions of the educational force: Kindergarten, Elementary, Special (Elementary), Junior High School, Senior High School, Administration, Personal Servive, and Professional Service.

The teachers in junior and senior high schools were classified according to the subject which they taught; and the per cent of secondary school teachers (not of the total educational force) which they comprised was computed. It was both impracticable and unnecessary to compute percentages for every one of the more than three hundred and fifty subjects taught, as given in List 5, and they were therefore grouped. List 6 gives the grouping. This was also arbitrarily made from the point of view of the teaching personnel. Under Trades were listed all the courses on manual training and industrial arts, as well as the new trade courses which have sprung up, but the home economics courses and sewing and cooking were given a separate grouping. This fact should be kept in mind in reading the graphs.

LIST 1

PERSONNEL OF MAINTENANCE *

1. Accountant
2. Adjuster
3. Assistant storekeeper
4. Auditor
5. Building manager
6. Buy order clerk
7. Cafeteria manager—café manager
8. Carpenter
9. Chief of inspection and maintenance—inspector of maintenance
10. Chauffeur
11. Clerk
12. Deputy auditor
13. Draftsman
14. Elevator operator

* This list is not complete.

15. Foreman of maintenance
16. Foreman of plumbers
17. Good housekeeping inspector
18. Head draftsman
19. Inspector of janitor service
20. Inspector of supplies
21. Inspector of transportation
22. Insurance and financial clerk
23. Janitor
24. Janitor-engineer
25. Painter
26. Photographer
27. Piano tuner
28. Plumber
29. Publicity agent
30. Purchasing clerk
31. Realty investigator
32. Specification writer
33. Stenographer
34. Stock accountant
35. Storekeeper
36. Supervisor of pay rolls
37. Truck driver

LIST 2

Personnel of Professional Service

1. Architect—supervisor of school architecture
2. Assistant director of educational research
3. Assistant director of elementary research
4. Assistant director of high school research
5. Assistant electrical engineer
6. Assistant heating and ventilating engineer
7. Assistant sanitary engineer
8. Assistant structural engineer
9. Assistant supervisor of construction
10. Assistant supervisor of psychology
11. Demonstrator
12. Director of educational research
13. Director of medical inspection
14. District medical supervisor
15. Electrical engineer
16. Engineer
17. Heating and ventilating engineer
18. Landscape gardener
19. Medical sanitation inspector
20. Office engineer
21. Research assistant

22. Research assistant to director of classics
23. Sanitary engineer
24. School psychologist
25. Statistician
26. Structural engineer
27. Supervisor of construction
28. Supervisor of health examination of employees
29. Supplies statistician

LIST 3

PERSONNEL OF PERSONAL SERVICE

1. Assistant director of medical inspection
2. Assistant director of nurses
3. Assistant librarian
4. Assistant supervisor of nurses
5. Assistant supervisor of school savings
6. Attendance officer
7. Attendance officer for juvenile courts
8. Attendance officer for street trades
9. Chief nurse
10. Coach
11. Community music
12. Coördinator
13. Corrective nutritionist
14. Dentist
15. Field nurse
16. Forum lecturer
17. Head coördinator
18. Junior placement officer
19. Librarian
20. Library and textbook clerk
21. Medical examiner
22. Medical inspector
23. Nutritionist
24. Nurse
25. Occupational therapy
26. Optometrist
27. Personal service
28. Physician
29. Placement officer
30. Reference librarian
31. Roentgenologist
32. School mother
33. Superintendent of libraries
34. Supervisor of placement
35. Supervisor of professors' children's interests
36. Supervisor of safety patrols

37. Supervisor of school savings
38. Supervisor of tuberculosis work
39. Supervisor of working children's interests
40. Supervising librarian
41. Traveling assistant librarian
42. Tuberculosis work
43. Visiting teacher
44. Work permits

LIST 4

ADMINISTRATION AND SUPERVISION

1. Assistant business manager
2. Assistant director of art
3. Assistant director of attendance
4. Assistant director of commercial education
5. Assistant director of compulsory education
6. Assistant director of examinations
7. Assistant director of forestry
8. Assistant director of health education
9. Assistant director of industrial arts
10. Assistant director of music
11. Assistant director of physical education and athletics
12. Assistant director of school extension
13. Assistant director of visual education
14. Assistant director of vocational education
15. Assistant supervisor of agriculture
16. Assistant supervisor of Americanization
17. Assistant supervisor of attendance
18. Assistant supervisor of commercial education
19. Assistant supervisor of crippled
20. Assistant supervisor of deaf
21. Assistant supervisor of drawing
22. Assistant supervisor of handicapped children
23. Assistant supervisor of home economics
24. Assistant supervisor of industrial arts
25. Assistant supervisor of kindergarten
26. Assistant supervisor of manual education
27. Assistant supervisor of music
28. Assistant supervisor of nature study
29. Assistant supervisor of orchestra
30. Assistant supervisor of penmanship
31. Assistant supervisor of physical education
32. Assistant supervisor of primary manual arts
33. Assistant supervisor of reserve officers training corps
34. Assistant supervisor of safety education
35. Assistant supervisor of salesmanship
36. Assistant supervisor of speech correction

37. Associate superintendent of education
38. Associate superintendent of junior high schools
39. Associate superintendent of organization of elementary schools
40. Associate superintendent of school buildings
41. Associate superintendent of school extension work
42. Associate superintendent of senior high schools
43. Associate superintendent of special education
44. Associate superintendent of supplies
45. Associate superintendent of teacher-training schools
46. Business manager
47. Controller
48. Dean of boys
49. Dean of girls
50. Director of American historical research
51. Director of Americanization
52. Director of art
53. Director of citizenship
54. Director of classics
55. Director of commercial education
56. Director of compulsory attendance—compulsory education
57. Director of course of study
58. Director of examinations
59. Director of foreign languages
60. Director of health education
61. Director of home economics
62. Director of industrial arts
63. Director of kindergarten education
64. Director of libraries
65. Director of music
66. Director of nurses
67. Director of plant operation
68. Director of part-time instruction
69. Director of physical education and athletics
70. Director of science
71. Director of school extension
72. Director of special education
73. Director of visual education
74. Director of vocational education
75. Head of agricultural center
76. Principal of elementary school
77. Principal of junior high school
78. Principal of normal school
79. Principal of senior high school
80. Principal of special school
81. Registrar
82. Secretary
83. Solicitor
84. Special supervisor of attendance

85. Superintendent of education
86. Superintendent of janitors
87. Superintendent of maintenance
88. Superintendent of plant operation
89. Superintendent of school buildings
90. Superintendent of supplies
91. Supervisor of agriculture
92. Supervisor of Americanization
93. Supervisor of art
94. Supervisor of attendance for special service
95. Supervisor of attendance for counseling
96. Supervisor of census and transfer
97. Supervisor of commercial education
98. Supervisor of corrective physical education
99. Supervisor of deaf and hard-of-hearing
100. Supervisor of drawing
101. Supervisor of employment
102. Supervisor of grades
103. Supervisor of handwriting
104. Supervisor of health
105. Supervisor of home economics
106. Supervisor of industrial arts
107. Supervisor of kindergarten
108. Supervisor of manual education
109. Supervisor of mechanical arts
110. Supervisor of mechanical drawing
111. Supervisor of modern languages
112. Supervisor of music
113. Supervisor of nature study
114. Supervisor of orchestra
115. Supervisor of penmanship
116. Supervisor of primary manual arts
117. Supervisor of psychology
118. Supervisor of reserve officers' training corps
119. Supervisor of safety education
120. Supervisor of salesmanship
121. Supervisor of school extension
122. Supervisor of science
123. Supervisor of special classes
124. Supervisor of special education
125. Supervisor of speech correction—improvement
126. Supervisor of state history (California)
127. Supervisor of vocational education
128. Supervisor of welfare centers
129. Treasurer

LIST 5

PUBLIC SCHOOL TEACHERS

1. Accountancy
2. Adjustment group
3. Advertising
4. Aëronautics
5. Agriculture
6. Algebra
7. Alterations
8. Americanization
9. Anatomy
10. Animal husbandry
11. Application
12. Applied English
13. Applied textiles
14. Applied textile mathematics
15. Applied textile design
16. Apprentice teachers
17. Architectural drafting
18. Architectural drawing
19. Architectural modeling
20. Architecture
21. Arithmetic
22. Art
23. Art appreciation
24. Art metal
25. Art needlework
26. Art weaving
27. Astronomy
28. Auto brake adjustment
29. Auto electrics—laboratory
30. Auto electrics—theory
31. Auto mechanics—auto repair
32. Auto theory
33. Auto upkeep
34. Bacteriology
35. Baking technology
36. Band
37. Basketry
38. Batik leather
39. Beauty culture
40. Bench work
41. Biology
42. Blind
43. Blue print reading
44. Bookbinding
45. Bookkeeping
46. Botany
47. Braille
48. Bricklaying
49. Building construction
50. Business methods
51. Cabinetmaking
52. Cable splicing
53. Café management—cafeteria
54. Card writing
55. Carpentry
56. Cartooning
57. Cement
58. Ceramics
59. Chemistry
60. Child study
61. China painting
62. Choral
63. Citizenship
64. Civics
65. Civil engineering
66. Civil service
67. Clay modeling
68. Cleaning (clothes)
69. Clog dancing
70. Clothing
71. Commerce
72. Commercial arithmetic
73. Commercial geography
74. Commercial law
75. Commercial subjects
76. Commercial telegraphy
77. Commodities
78. Concrete construction
79. Construction machine work
80. Construction drawing
81. Continuation
82. Cooking
83. Corrective nutrition
84. Corrective physical education
85. Crafts
86. Cripples
87. Critic teacher
88. Current events
89. Dancing
90. Deaf

91. Debating
92. Decoration
93. Democracy
94. Dental hygiene
95. Design
96. Detail drawing
97. Detailing (stock)
98. Dietetics
99. Domestic science
100. Drama
101. Dramatics
102. Dressmaking
103. Economics
104. Education
105. Electricity
106. Electrical construction
107. Electrical lighting
108. Electrical wiring
109. Elocution
110. Elementary business methods
111. Engineering
112. Engine testing
113. English
114. English to foreigners
115. Esperanto
116. Estimating
117. Expression
118. Fancy spotting
119. Figure drawing
120. Finance
121. First aid
122. Floriculture
123. Flower making
124. Foods
125. Folk dancing
126. Forge shop
127. Free-hand decorating
128. Free-hand drawing
129. French
130. French draping
131. Garment design
132. Gas and electric welding
133. Gas engine mechanics
134. General science
135. General mathematics
136. General textiles
137. Geography
138. Geology
139. Geometry
140. German
141. Glee club
142. Grade teacher
143. Hand composition
144. Handwork
145. Hair and skin
146. Harmony
147. Health
148. History
149. History of art
150. History of education
151. History of music
152. Home economics
153. Home gardening
154. Homemaking
155. Home nursing
156. Home teachers of Americanization
157. Home teachers of English and citizenship
158. Home thrift
159. Horticulture
160. Household arts
161. House painting
162. Hygiene
163. Illustrating
164. Industrial arts
165. Industrial processes
166. Industries
167. Instrument making
168. Interior decorating
169. Ironwork
170. Italian
171. Janitor engineering
172. Jewelry
173. Joinery
174. Journalism
175. Kindergarten
176. Laboratory assistant
177. Lace making
178. Landscape gardening
179. Latin
180. Laundry work
181. Law
182. Lead work
183. Leather
184. Lettering

185. Library craft
186. Life sketching
187. Linotyping
188. Lip reading
189. Literature—belles-lettres
190. Logic
191. Machine bookkeeping
192. Machine calculation
193. Machine construction
194. Machine design
195. Machine knitting
196. Machine operation
197. Machine shop
198. Manual training
199. Marketing of textiles
200. Mathematics
201. Meat cutting
202. Mechanical drafting
203. Mechanical drawing
204. Mechanics
205. Mechanics of materials
206. Mechanism
207. Metal work
208. Mill cabinet
209. Millinery
210. Milling
211. Military science
212. Mineralogy
213. Mining
214. Monotyping
215. Music
216. Music appreciation
217. Nature study
218. Navigation
219. Needlework
220. Newspaper
221. Non-curricular
222. Normal work
223. Norse
224. Novelty
225. Nursing
226. Nutrition
227. Occupational therapy
228. Occupations
229. Office practice
230. Oil painting
231. Open-air class
232. Opera

233. Orchestra
234. Organ
235. Ornamental ironwork
236. Orthopedic classes
237. Oxy-acetylene welding
238. Pacific rim
239. Paper hanging
240. Parental education
241. Pattern making
242. P.B.X. telephone operation
243. Pedagogy
244. Penmanship
245. Personal hygiene
246. Personal service
247. Philology
248. Philosophy
249. Phonography
250. Photography
251. Physical education
252. Physics
253. Physics and chemistry of textiles
254. Physiography
255. Physiology
256. Piano
257. Pipe fitting
258. Plant science
259. Plastering, plain and ornamental
260. Plastic art
261. Play writing
262. Plumbing
263. Plumbing layout
264. Political economy
265. Poster
266. Posture
267. Pottery
268. Power machine
269. Power sewing
270. Practical electricity
271. Pressing
272. Press work
273. Psychology
274. Public speaking
275. Quantity foods
276. Radio
277. Rapid promotion class
278. Raw materials of commerce

279. Reading
280. Records
281. Reed craft
282. Reed furniture weaving
283. Restoration class
284. Retail selling
285. Roof framing
286. R.O.T.C. officers class
287. R.O.T.C. rifle practice
288. R.R. station accountancy
289. Salesmanship
290. Scene painting
291. School paper
292. Sewing
293. Sheet metal
294. Ship design and construction
295. Shoemaking
296. Shop
297. Shop assistant
298. Shorthand
299. Show card (poster)
300. Short story
301. Sign painting
302. Sight conservation
303. Sight singing
304. Slide rule
305. Sloyd
306. Social aspects of education
307. Social problems
308. Social studies
309. Sociology
310. Soda dispensing
311. Smithing
312. Spanish
313. Special classes
314. Special catering
315. Speech correction
316. Stage costuming
317. Stagecraft
318. Stage electrics
319. Steam
320. Steel design
321. Steel square
322. Stenography

323. Sticker (carpentry)
324. Stock billing
325. Supervised study
326. Surveying
327. Swedish
328. Swimming
329. Tailoring
330. Telegraphy
331. Telephone operating
332. Theme reader
333. Theory of music
334. Theory of teaching
335. Thrift
336. Tile setting
337. Topographical drawing
338. Trade drawing
339. Trade sewing
340. Transportation
341. Traveling teacher for crippled children
342. Traveling teacher of state (California) history
343. Trigonometry
344. Teacher in hospital wards
345. Typewriting
346. Ungraded
347. Upholstery
348. Violin
349. Vise shop
350. Visualization
351. Vocal music—voice
352. Vocational arts
353. Vocational cookery
354. Vocations
355. Vulcanizing
356. Weaving
357. Welding
358. Wheel and axle alignment
359. Wholesome living
360. Wicker shop
361. Wind instruments
362. Wood carving
363. Woodwork
364. Zoölogy

LIST 6

GROUPING OF THE SECONDARY SCHOOL SUBJECTS REPORTED IN THIS STUDY

1. Aëronautics—Aviation
2. Agriculture
    Animal husbandry
    Floriculture
    Horticulture
    Home gardening
    Landscape gardening
3. Architecture
    Architectural drafting
    Architectural drawing
    Architectural modeling
4. Arts and Drawing
    Art appreciation
    Art metal
    Art needlework
    Art weaving
    Batik leather
    Card writing
    Cartooning
    Ceramics
    China painting
    Clay modeling
    Crafts
    Decoration
    Design
    Detail drawing
    Figure drawing
    Free-hand drawing
    Handwork
    History of art
    Illustrating
    Jewelry
    Lettering
    Life sketching
    Oil painting
    Painting
    Plastic art
    Poster
    Pottery
    Related art
    Scene painting
    Show card
    Wood carving
5. Astronomy

6. Biological Sciences
    Anatomy
    Bacteriology
    Biology
    Botany
    Nature study
    Plant science
    Zoölogy
7. Chemistry
8. Civics
    Americanization
    Citizenship
    Democracy
    Economics
    Pacific rim
    Political economy
    Political science
9. Commercial Subjects
    Accountancy
    Advertising
    Auditing
    Bookkeeping
    Business methods
    Business organization
    Commerce
    Commercial arithmetic
    Commercial geography
    Commercial law
    Commodities
    Detailing
    Economic geography
    Estimating
    Finance
    Industrial processes
    Industries
    Junior business practice
    Office practice
    Penmanship
    Phonography
    Raw materials of commerce
    Retail selling
    Salesmanship
    Shorthand
    Stenography
    Stock billing

9. Commercial Subjects (*Cont'd*)
    Textiles
        Applied textile mathematics
        Applied textile design
        Applied textiles
        General textiles
        Physics and chemistry of
    Typewriting
10. English
    Applied English
    Belles-lettres
    Drama
    Dramatics
    Elocution
    English to foreigners
    Expression
    Forum lectures
    Journalism
    Literature
    Newspaper
    Philology
    Play writing
    Public speaking
    Reading
    Short story
    Speech correction
    Spelling
    Theme reader
11. Engineering
    Civil engineering
    Engine testing
    Mining
    Navigation
    Ship design and construction
    Surveying
12. Esperanto
13. French
14. General science
15. Geography—physiography
16. Geology—mineralogy
17. German
18. History
    Current events
    Traveling teacher of state history

19. Hygiene
    Corrective physical education
    First aid
    Health
    Home nursing
    Orthopedic classes
    Personal hygiene
    Physiology
    Wholesome living
20. Home Economics
    Baking technology
    Café management
    Cafeteria
    Clothing
    Cooking
    Corrective nutrition
    Dietetics
    Dressmaking
    Foods
    French draping
    Garment design
    Homemaking
    Home thrift
    Household arts
    Household science
    Interior decorating
    Millinery
    Needlework
    Nutrition
    Quantity foods
    Sewing
    Special catering
21. Italian
22. Laboratory Assistant
23. Latin and Greek
24. Logic
25. Mathematics
    Algebra
    Arithmetic
    General mathematics
    Geometry
    Slide rule
    Trigonometry
26. Music
    Appreciation
    Band
    Glee club

26. Music (*Cont'd*)
    Harmony
    History of music
    Opera
    Orchestra
    Organ
    Piano
    Sight singing
    Theory of music
    Violin
    Vocal music
    Voice
27. Norse
28. Occupations
29. Physical Training
    Athletics
    Clog dancing
    Folk dancing
    Military science
    R.O.T.C. officers class
    R.O.T.C. rifle practice
    Social dancing
    Swimming
30. Physics
31. Sociology
    Social problems
    Social studies
32. Spanish
33. Swedish
34. Trades
    Auto mechanics
        Auto brake adjustment
        Auto   electrics — labora-
           tory
        Auto electrics—theory
        Auto mechanics
        Auto repair
        Auto theory
        Auto upkeep
    Beauty culture
    Building construction
    Carpentry
        Cabinetmaking
        Milling cabinet
        Sticking
    Cement
        Concrete construction

34. Trades (*Cont'd*)
    Cleaning
        Fancy spotting
        Pressing
    Electricity
        Lighting
        Practical electricity
        Wiring
    Flower making
    Gas engine mechanics
    Hair and skin
    House painting
    Janitor engineering
    Lace making
    Laundry work
    Machine shop—machine op-
       eration
    Meat cutting
    Mechanical arts
        Blue print reading
        Forge shop
        Ironwork
        Joinery
        Lead work
        Leather
        Metal work
        Pattern making
        Sheet metal
        Shop assistant
        Steam
        Steel design
        Steel square
        Vise shop
    Mechanics
        Construction drawing
        Machine construction
        Machine design
        Machine operation
        Mechanical drafting
        Mechanical drawing
        Mechanics
        Mechanism
    Mechanics of materials
    Novelty
    Paper hanging
    Photography
    Plastering
    Plumbing—pipe fitting

34. Trades (*Cont'd*)
    Power machine—power sewing
    Printing
      Bookbinding
      Hand composition
      Linotype
      Monotype
      Presswork
    Radio
    Reed craft
      Basketry
      Reed furniture weaving
    Roof framing
    R.R. station accountancy
    Shampooing
    Shoemaking
    Sign painting
    Smithing
    Soda dispensing

34. Trades (*Cont'd*)
    Stagecraft
      Costuming
      Stage electricity
    Tailoring
    Telegraphy
    Telephone operation—
      P.B.X. tel. operation
    Tile setting
    Trade drawing
    Trade sewing
    Transportation
    Upholstering
    Vulcanizing
    Welding
      Oxy-acetylene welding
      Gas and electric
    Woodwork
35. Thrift

CHAPTER IV

CROSS SECTION OF THE EDUCATIONAL OCCUPATIONS IN 1928

TOTAL SYSTEM

Table 3 and Chart 1 give a picture of the educational force of fourteen public school systems. The elementary teachers constitute almost half of the total number. If to the regular elementary teachers are added the special elementary teachers, the number amounts to more than one-half. And if to this number are added the kindergarten teachers, we find that the teachers of children up to the seventh or ninth grade (depending on whether the system has junior high schools) constitute 63.15 per cent of the total educational staff.

Kindergarten.—In the kindergarten the range is from 2.58 per cent to 7.72 per cent. The per cent of kindergarten teachers does not seem to depend on the size of the city. The largest city and the smallest city studied, New York and Warren, Pennsylvania, have practically the same per cent; whereas the second smallest city, Waltham, Massachusetts, has the largest per cent.

Elementary.—With respect to the per cent of special teachers there is considerable variation from one city to another—4.51 per cent to 25.15 per cent. These figures, however, are not strictly comparable, for the different cities reported them in different ways. Some cities have few or no junior high schools, and the seventh and eighth grade teachers are therefore included in the elementary schools. If these grades are departmentalized the teachers are included under the head of special teachers; otherwise under the regular elementary staff. The total for the elementary teachers probably gives a better picture than either the grade teachers or special teachers alone. The proportion ranges from 41.42 per cent in Los Angeles to 70.75 per cent in Newark.

Junior High.—Of the thirteen cities studied, four—Boston, Buffalo, St. Louis, and Warren—had no junior high schools.

22

TABLE 3

Number and Per Cent of Persons in Each Division of the Educational Force for the Year 1928 *

City	Total Number	Kindergarten		Elementary		Special		Per Cent Total Elementary (Combined Elementary and Special)	Junior High School	
		Number	Per Cent	Number	Per Cent	Number	Per Cent		Number	Per Cent
Baltimore	3,161	120.0	3.80	1,665.0	52.67	217.00	6.87	59.54	534.00	16.89
Los Angeles	9,770	446.0	4.56	3,153.5	32.28	892.67	9.14	41.42	1,187.83	12.16
Philadelphia	9,033	380.0	4.21	4,340.0	48.04	1,006.00	11.14	59.18	1,257.00	13.91
Pittsburgh	3,449	165.0	4.78	821.5	23.82	771.50	22.36	46.18	179.00	5.19
Providence	1,487	63.0	4.24	566.0	38.06	374.00	25.15	63.21	179.00	4.10
Warren	125	4.0	3.20	66.0	52.80	8.00	6.40	59.20	61.00	0
Boston	4,575	305.0	6.67	2,392.5	52.29	453.50	9.91	62.20	0	0
Buffalo	3,625	159.5	4.40	1,527.5	42.14	787.00	21.71	63.85	0	0
Cleveland	5,041	205.0	4.07	1,983.0	39.34	662.00	13.13	52.47	1,127.00	22.35
Newark	2,106	130.0	6.17	1,363.0	64.72	127.00	6.03	70.75	73.00	3.47
New York	30,451	1,055.0	3.46	17,409.0	57.17	2,046.00	6.72	63.85	2,901.00	9.53
St. Louis	3,120	216.0	6.92	1,972.5	63.22	207.00	6.63	69.85	0	0
Waltham	285	22.0	7.72	91.0	31.93	50.00	17.54	49.47	44.50	15.62
San Francisco	2,485	64.0	2.58	1,315.0	59.92	112.00	4.51	64.43	230.00	9.25
Total Number	78,713	3,334.5		38,665.5		7,713.67			7,594.33	
Total Per Cent			4.24		49.11		9.80			9.65

City	Senior High School		Administration		Personal		Professional		Per Cent Total High School (Combined Junior and Senior High Schools)
	Number	Per Cent	Number	Per Cent	Number	Per Cent	Number	Per Cent	
Baltimore	343.00	10.85	244.0	7.72	32.00	1.01	6.0	.19	27.74
Los Angeles	2,965.00	30.35	606.0	6.20	479.00	4.90	40.0	.41	42.51
Philadelphia	1,257.00	13.91	388.0	4.30	388.00	4.30	17.0	.19	27.82
Pittsburgh	957.00	27.74	259.0	7.52	292.00	8.47	4.0	.12	32.93
Providence	262.67	17.67	92.0	6.19	61.33	4.12	7.0	.47	21.77
Warren	40.00	32.00	7.0	5.60	0	0	0	0	32.00
Boston	922.50	20.17	319.0	6.97	179.50	3.92	3.0	.07	20.17
Buffalo	804.00	22.18	222.0	6.12	90.00	2.48	35.0	.97	22.18
Cleveland	701.00	13.91	351.0	6.96	8.00	.16	4.0	.08	36.26
Newark	300.00	14.24	75.0	3.56	37.00	1.76	4.0	.05	17.71
New York	5,153.00	16.92	1,488.5	4.89	395.00	1.30	4.0	.01	26.45
St. Louis	450.00	14.42	195.5	6.27	67.00	2.15	12.0	.39	14.42
Waltham	33.00	11.58	37.0	12.98	4.00	1.40	3.5	1.23	27.20
San Francisco	525.00	21.13	289.0	9.62					30.38
Total Number	14,713.17		4,522.5		2,052.83		136.5		
Total Per Cent		18.69		5.75		2.58		.17	

* Data were obtained from directories, pay rolls, or board minutes of the cities. See Table 1 for the actual year studied for each city.

Some of the cities have only a few junior high schools and others have many. In Newark only 3.5 per cent of the teachers are teaching in junior high school; in Providence only 4 per cent; in Cleveland 22 per cent.

Senior High.—The senior high school should be viewed from the standpoint of whether or not there are junior high schools in the city. Where the senior high schools include four grades, the percentage of teachers is naturally higher than it is where they have only three grades. Thus Boston and Buffalo, with no junior high schools, have a high percentage of teachers in senior high school. On the other hand, St. Louis, which also has

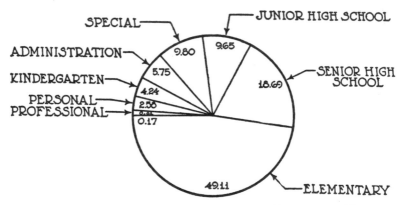

CHART 1. PERCENTAGE GRAPH OF THE EDUCATIONAL FORCE OF THE FOURTEEN CITIES STUDIED, 1928
(Based on Table 3)

no junior high school, has a very low percentage of teachers in the senior high school, and Los Angeles, which has a large junior high school system, has the largest percentage of teachers in senior high school of all the thirteen cities.

The total percentage of elementary teachers compared with the total percentage of high school teachers is probably indicative of the variety of subjects offered in the high schools. A wide variety to suit all abilities and interests probably has more holding power over children than a more rigid, classical curriculum, although methods of teaching, of course, have their influence also. Los Angeles has a larger percentage of teachers in the high schools than in the elementary schools. The original data show that Los Angeles offers more than 200 subjects, ranging from clog dancing and beauty culture to Latin and law. On the other hand, Pittsburgh, which has only 10 per cent more teachers in elementary schools than in high schools, offers less than 60 subjects. St. Louis has 55 per cent more teachers in elementary schools than in high schools and offers between 30 and 40 subjects. Inasmuch as these are all large systems, the variety of subjects would not be influenced by the size of the class. A city as small as Warren, where the total educational staff is only 125, would, of necessity, have to limit the variety of subjects offered.

Administration and Supervision.—The range in administration and supervision is from 3.56 per cent to 12.98 per cent. Neither the lowest, Newark, nor the highest, Waltham, is among the twelve largest cities. The largest city, New York, and the smallest, Warren, have almost the same percentage. Thus from the few cases studied it would seem that the size of the city had little to do with the per cent of the staff in administration and supervision.

Secondary Schools

Chart 2, based on the summary presented in Table 8, page 39, gives a picture of the secondary schools in 1928. English has by far the greatest number of teachers in the secondary school system, 18.37 per cent of the total secondary school teachers.

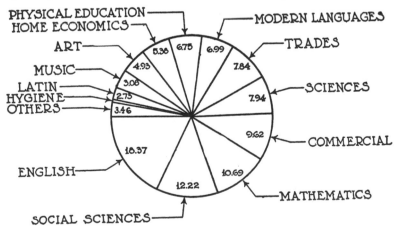

Chart 2. Percentage Graph of the Secondary School Teachers of the Fourteen Cities Studied, 1928

(Based on Table 8)

Social science and mathematics and the commercial subjects come next. Sciences and the trades are 2 per cent less than the commercial subjects. The number of teachers of home economics is just about half that of mathematics. Latin involves 2.73 per cent of the total and hygiene only 0.57 per cent. In a few subjects, such as astronomy and geology, the percentage is too small to show on the graph.

CONCLUSIONS

The following conclusions may be drawn for the thirteen cities studied:

1. The elementary school teachers constitute more than half of the educational force.

2. The percentage of kindergarten teachers does not seem to depend on the size of the city.

3. Junior high schools have grown rapidly, but there are still some cities where they have not been introduced.

4. The proportion of high school teachers to elementary school teachers ranges from one to four to one to one.

5. The percentage of persons in administration does not seem to depend on the size of the city.

6. In the secondary schools, English, the social sciences, mathematics, and the commercial subjects have the largest number of teachers, with English much in the lead.

7. Latin and hygiene are among the subjects with the fewest teachers. Astronomy and geology are now included in but very few schools.

CHAPTER V

TRENDS OF THE EDUCATIONAL OCCUPATIONS FROM
1898 TO 1928

For the purposes of vocational guidance it is not only important to know the present status of each of the educational occupations but it is equally important to know the past trends. Merely stating that, according to the cities studied, science teachers constitute at present 8 per cent of all secondary school teachers is of little significance without the additional fact that in 1898 they constituted more than 17 per cent and have been steadily decreasing ever since. And if to the information about the present status and past trends can be added such interpretation concerning probable causes as will provide a fairly safe estimate of future trends, the data will be of still greater value.

Chapter IV has pictured the present status. This chapter deals with the past trends and their probable causes in an attempt to estimate future trends for the vocational guidance of prospective teachers.

The data which show these trends came principally from the school directories of 1898, 1908, 1918, and 1928. Where the directories were not available the data were obtained from pay rolls or minutes of the board of education. The sources give the name and position of each member of the administrative force and the name of each teacher and the grade or subjects taught.

TOTAL SYSTEM

Chart 3, based on the summary tabulation of the data (Table 7), shows the trends in the main divisions of the educational force by decades from 1898 to 1928. Chart 4 shows the change that has taken place in each of these divisions during the total period.

Elementary.—The proportion of teachers in elementary schools declined rapidly from 1908 to 1928. This decline is probably due to the three causes listed on the following pages.

27

1. Specialization, in the elementary school, which has reduced the number of general teachers and increased the number of special teachers. The special teachers include teachers of un-

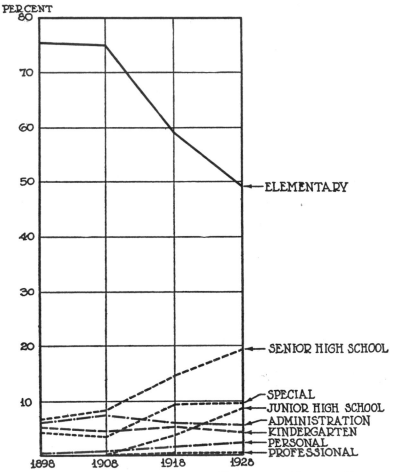

PERCENT

CHART 3. PERCENTAGE CHANGE IN THE EDUCATIONAL FORCE BY DECADES
FROM 1898 TO 1928
(Based on Table 7)

graded classes, adjustment classes, classes for the deaf, blind, crippled, and others, as well as teachers of music, art, etc. These teachers are drawn from the elementary force.

2. Rise of new groups and increase in the number of senior and junior high school teachers. Since the total per cent can

be only one hundred, a marked increase in any group or addition of another group must mean a decrease somewhere. This decrease in per cent occurred in the elementary school teachers.

3. Rise of junior high school. With the advent of the junior high school the number of grades in the elementary school was

TABLE 4

NUMBER AND PER CENT OF PERSONS IN EACH DIVISION OF THE EDUCATIONAL FORCE FOR THE YEAR 1898 *

CITY	TOTAL NUM-BER	KINDERGARTEN		ELEMENTARY		SPECIAL	
		Num-ber	Per Cent	Num-ber	Per Cent	Num-ber	Per Cent
Los Angeles	480	82	17.08	314.0	65.42	10.0	2.08
Philadelphia	3,287	192	5.84	2,601.0	79.13	101.0	3.07
Pittsburgh	920	14	1.52	745.0	80.98	41.0	4.46
Providence	605	29	4.79	366.5	60.66	68.0	11.24
Warren	39	0	0	30.0	76.92	2.5	6.41
Total Number.....	5,331	317	— —	4,056.5	— —	222.5	— —
Total Per Cent	— —	— —	5.95	— —	76.09	— —	4.17

CITY	SENIOR HIGH SCHOOL		ADMINIS-TRATION		PERSONAL		PROFES-SIONAL	
	Num-ber	Per Cent	Num-ber	Per Cent	Num-ber	Per Cent	Num-ber	Per Cent
Los Angeles	36.0	7.50	38.0	7.92	0	0	0	0
Philadelphia	182.5	5.55	210.5	6.41	0	0	0	0
Pittsburgh	54.0	5.87	54.0	5.87	12	1.30	0	0
Providence	86.0	14.21	54.5	8.93	1	.17	0	0
Warren	6.0	15.38	.5	1.28	0	0	0	0
Total Number.....	364.5	— —	357.5	— —	13	— —	0	— —
Total Per Cent	— —	6.84	— —	6.71	— —	.24	— —	0

* Data were obtained from directories, pay rolls, or board minutes of the cities.

reduced from eight to six, with a consequent diminution of teaching force allotted to the elementary school.

Special Elementary.—There was a marked increase in the number of special elementary teachers during the decade 1908-18. Since then, however, there has been little change. Probably many of the special teachers were at that time in the seventh and eighth grades and are now classified as in junior high school, though still in the same grades. It is possible that the percentage of special teachers in the lower grades has increased during this period even though the data do not show it. However, the range was so wide and the trend varied so much that little can be said.

Kindergarten.—The percentage of kindergarten teachers has remained practically the same since 1898, although it varies

TABLE 5

NUMBER AND PER CENT OF PERSONS IN EACH DIVISION OF THE EDUCATIONAL
FORCE FOR THE YEAR 1908 *

CITY	TOTAL NUM- BER	KINDERGARTEN		ELEMENTARY		SPECIAL	
		Num- ber	Per Cent	Num- ber	Per Cent	Num- ber	Per Cent
Baltimore	1,828	44.0	2.41	1,511.0	82.66	54.0	2.95
Los Angeles	1,085	110.0	10.14	685.5	63.19	71.0	6.54
Philadelphia	4,375	203.0	4.73	3,381.0	76.85	81.0	1.89
Pittsburgh	1,263	45.0	3.56	924.5	73.20	83.0	6.57
Providence	744	53.5	7.19	476.5	64.05	37.0	4.97
Warren	56	0.0	0.00	36.0	64.29	9.5	16.96
Total Number.....	9,351	455.5	--	7,014.5	--	335.5	--
Total Per Cent	--	--	4.87	--	75.01	--	3.59

CITY	SENIOR HIGH SCHOOL		ADMINIS- TRATION		PERSONAL		PROFES- SIONAL	
	Num- ber	Per Cent	Num- ber	Per Cent	Num- ber	Per Cent	Num- ber	Per Cent
Baltimore	107	5.85	100.0	5.47	12	.66	0	0
Los Angeles	131	12.07	81.5	7.51	6	.55	0	0
Philadelphia	341	7.94	325.0	7.57	44	1.02	0	0
Pittsburgh	71	5.62	122.5	9.70	16	1.27	1	.08
Providence	106	14.25	69.0	9.27	2	.27	0	0
Warren	10	17.86	.5	.89	0	0	0	0
Total Number.....	766	--	698.5	--	80	--	1	--
Total Per Cent	--	8.19	--	7.47	--	.86	--	.01

* Data were obtained from the directories, pay rolls, or board minutes of the cities. See Table 1 for the actual year studied in each city.

widely in the different systems studied. In some cities it consistently increased and in others as consistently decreased; in still others it increased during one period and decreased during another.

Junior High.—The junior high schools came in during the decade 1908-18. There were none in 1908 and only a few by 1918. The largest growth has been since 1918. By 1928 the teachers in junior high schools constituted almost 10 per cent of the educational force.

Senior High.—There is a marked rise in the percentage of senior high school teachers in spite of the fact that in many

TABLE 6

NUMBER AND PER CENT OF PERSONS IN EACH DIVISION OF THE EDUCATIONAL FORCE FOR THE YEAR 1918 *

CITY	TOTAL NUMBER	KINDERGARTEN		ELEMENTARY		SPECIAL	
		Number	Per Cent	Number	Per Cent	Number	Per Cent
Baltimore	2,294	50.0	2.18	1,604.0	69.93	235.0	10.24
Cleveland	3,529	172.5	4.89	1,864.1	52.82	217.9	6.18
Los Angeles	3,079	268.0	8.70	1,565.0	50.83	408.0	13.26
Philadelphia	6,272	264.0	4.21	4,099.0	65.38	487.0	7.74
Pittsburgh	2,711	193.0	7.12	1,424.0	52.53	377.5	13.93
Providence	999	59.0	5.91	586.5	58.70	99.0	9.91
Warren	91	.0	0	64.0	70.34	6.0	6.59
Total Number...	18,975	1,006.5	--	11,206.6	--	1,830.4	--
Total Per Cent ..	--	--	5.30	--	59.06	--	9.65

CITY	JUNIOR HIGH SCHOOL		SENIOR HIGH SCHOOL		ADMINISTRATION		PERSONAL		PROFESSIONAL	
	Number	Per Cent	Number	Per Cent	Number	Per Cent	Number	Per Cent	Number	Per Cent
Baltimore	0	0	221.0	9.63	151	6.58	32.0	1.40	1	.04
Cleveland	642	18.19	428.0	12.13	196	5.55	8.5	.24	0	0
Los Angeles	0	0	566.0	18.38	210	6.82	58.0	1.88	4	.13
Philadelphia ...	36	.57	954.0	15.21	274	4.37	158.0	2.52	0	0
Pittsburgh	70	2.58	372.0	13.72	180	6.64	92.5	3.41	2	.07
Providence	0	0	169.5	16.97	84	8.41	1.0	.10	0	0
Warren	0	0	17.0	18.68	4	4.39	0	0	0	0
Total Number ..	748	--	2,727.5	--	1,099	--	350.0	--	7	--
Total Per Cent.	--	3.94	--	14.37	--	5.79	--	1.85	--	.04

* Data were obtained from the directories, pay rolls, or board minutes of the cities.

systems one grade has been taken away from the senior high school and placed in the junior high school, and in a few cities a grade has been withdrawn to be added to the junior college. An important question is whether this increase is permanent or only temporary.

For the past twenty years the trend has been away from the old classical curriculum, suited to the interests and ability of the few, toward a more diversified curriculum which would

TABLE 7

PER CENT OF PERSONS IN EACH DIVISION OF THE EDUCATIONAL FORCE AT
TEN-YEAR INERVALS, 1898 TO 1928 *

(A Summary of Tables 3 to 6)

DIVISION	1898	1908	1918	1928
Kindergarten	5.95	4.87	5.30	4.24
Elementary	76.09	75.01	59.06	49.11
Special (Elementary)	4.17	3.59	9.65	9.80
Junior High School	0	0	3.94	9.65
Senior High School	6.84	8.19	14.37	18.69
Administration	6.71	7.47	5.79	5.75
Personal	.24	.86	1.85	2.58
Professional	0	.01	.04	.17

* See Table 1 for the actual years studied for each city.

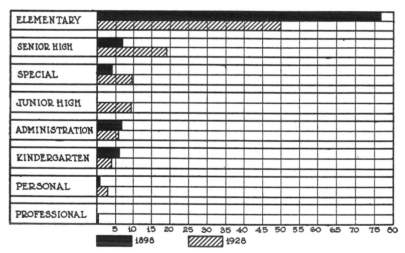

CHART 4. PERCENTAGE CHANGE IN TOTAL EDUCATIONAL FORCE, 1898 TO 1928
(Based on Table 7)

appeal to many interests and abilities. Whether the democratic idea that all persons should have the opportunity to obtain a secondary education caused a change in the curriculum or whether the change in the curriculum resulted in greater numbers remaining in school for further education is of little moment in this study. The factors probably interacted upon each other. The result is that the percentage of teachers needed to teach high school subjects has been steadily increasing during the past twenty years.

Administration and Supervision.—The administrative and supervisory division of education has kept almost the same proportionate relationship to the rest of the staff that it had in 1898. The percentage has dropped slightly. It seems to have been practically stabilized by 1918. In both 1918 and 1928 the range was slight in the cities studied.

Personal Service.—In 1898 there were only a few cities with educational officers giving personal service. They consisted for the most part of attendance officers. By 1908 all of the cities studied, except Warren, had officers giving this service. By 1928 the personal service group comprised 2.5 per cent of the total educational force.

Professional Service.—The group of professional workers, such as psychologist, research worker, and statistician, had only one representative in 1908 in the cities studied. By 1918 three of the six cities had workers in this field. By 1928 twelve of the thirteen cities had such workers. They are still only a fraction of one per cent of the educational force.

CONCLUSIONS CONCERNING ELEMENTARY SCHOOLS

The following conclusions may be drawn from the data for the thirteen cities studied:

1. The percentage of elementary teachers has declined rapidly during the past thirty years.

2. The percentage of kindergarten teachers and the percentage of administrators and supervisors have remained practically the same during this period.

3. The percentage in the other divisions has been increasing.

4. The junior high schools began during the decade 1908-18. They have grown rapidly, though in 1928 there were still some cities where they had not yet been introduced.

5. The personal service division had already started in 1898, and by 1918 almost all the cities had such service.

6. The professional service division was just beginning in 1908 and is not yet universal.

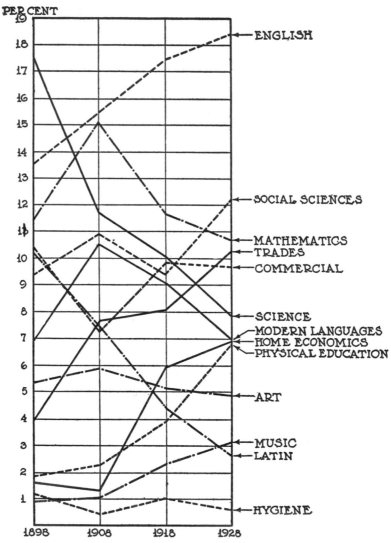

CHART 5. PERCENTAGE CHANGE IN THE SECONDARY SCHOOL TEACHERS BY
DECADES FROM 1898 TO 1928

(Based on Table 8)

SECONDARY SCHOOLS

Chart 5, based on the summary in Table 8, gives a picture of the changes in the more important school subjects by decades from 1898 to 1928. Chart 6 shows the change that has taken place in each of the major subjects during the total period. In order thoroughly to understand these changes and their impli-

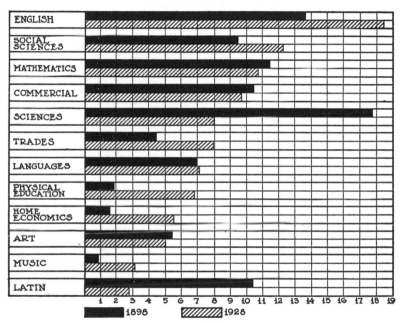

CHART 6. PERCENTAGE CHANGE IN THE SECONDARY SCHOOL TEACHERS OF THE FOURTEEN CITIES STUDIED, 1898 TO 1928

(Based on Table 8)

cations for the future it will be wise to note briefly some of the influences which are operating on the secondary school curriculum.

Influences Acting on the Curriculum.—In *Keeping Pace with the Advancing Curriculum* the National Educational Association [1] cites four important influences that have been operating on the secondary school curriculum. The teaching personnel is, of course, also affected by these factors.

[1] *Keeping Pace with the Advancing Curriculum,* pp. 112-13. National Education Association Research Bulletin.

1. *Rapidity of change.* The old curricula were based on a more or less stable world, where the older generation wished to pass on to the younger generation what it had learned. To-day the body of knowledge is changing so rapidly that it is not so much information as a point of view and ability to change with a changing world that is necessary for the younger generation.

The new objective has a strong influence on the content subjects, such as geography, history, mathematics, causing changes in method of presentation and minimizing their place in the curriculum.

2. *Complexity of modern life.* At first the complexity of the modern age was reflected in the great variety of new subjects which were added to the curriculum. Then educators realized that the curriculum was being cut up into so many small parts that the children were learning little of any of them, and as a result the compulsory subjects were limited and a wide variety of electives was offered. This required that courses stand on their proved value of usefulness to modern life.

3. *Increases in attendance and pupil heterogeneity.* "The rate of increase of public high school enrollments, 1890-1924, was approximately twenty times that of the total population." [2] Originally secondary education functioned principally as a step to college and was open only to those of high ability. With the increase in numbers, however, there was a marked widening of the range in pupil abilities and interests. The result has been a wider range in elective subjects, fewer required subjects, and a reduction in the percentage of pupils taking the subjects usually considered as more difficult to master, such as higher mathematics, sciences, Latin, and modern languages. There has been a large increase in the number of pupils studying the trades, home economics, and commercial subjects.

4. *Advances in educational science and psychology.* Numerous scientific studies of results in education have put a premium on those subjects which can scientifically prove their value. This naturally brings up the question of desired values.

To these four influences should be added a fifth:

5. *A slowly changing philosophy of education.* Several generations ago the aim of education was to prepare the child to

[2] *Biennial Survey of Education*, 1924-26, p. 135.

fit into a future static society through a knowledge of the past experiences of the race. Now the philosophy is gradually changing to a conception of education which holds that present living in a changing world is the best preparation for future living in a changing world.

This philosophy is opposed to a curriculum with water-tight compartments. It advocates such general courses as general science, general mathematics, general social studies, or no fixed courses at all. Since this trend is only in its infancy, the general courses will probably grow enormously in the next few years, and the separate courses in science, mathematics, and the social sciences will probably decline. On the other hand, the "activity" courses, such as music, arts, industrial arts, home economics, and physical education, are likely to receive stimulus.

CHAPTER VI

DEMAND AND SUPPLY

THE DEMAND

In order that the data be made more valuable in showing actual demand, the total number of secondary school teachers was found for the years 1898 and 1908 from the reports of the Commissioner of Education and the total for 1918 from the *Biennial Survey of Education*. Inasmuch as the *Biennial Survey* giving the data for 1928 had not yet been published, the report for 1926 was used. To these totals the per cents from Tables 11 to 36 were applied in order to obtain the approximate number of teachers in each subject. The results are given in Table 8. The number of teachers in each subject for each decade was subtracted from the number in the same subject in the previous decade, for the approximate increase or decrease of teachers in that subject during the ten-year period. Table 9 gives these figures. These numbers must be taken as only approximate, for they were derived from the application of per cents obtained from a small number of cities to the totals for public and private schools of the country as a whole. Nevertheless, the estimate is indicative of findings to be expected from more precise methods, and is of value in the present attempt to ascertain trends.

These numbers give only the total additions to the force; they entirely leave out of consideration replacements of those who for one reason or another have left the occupation for other employment, those who have retired, and those who have died. They make no allowance for those who have transferred from one department to another or have changed from teaching to administrative or supervisory positions. These factors would all have a tendency to raise the numbers given.

Elsbree gives approximate figures for the turnover of teachers in the different subjects in the state of New York.[1] The figures

[1] Elsbree, W. S., *Teacher Turnover in the Cities and Villages of New York State*, p. 21.

38

for science, Latin, and modern languages are the highest, being
17.13 per cent, 14.29 per cent, and 12.8 per cent, respectively.
The larger turnover would have the effect of making the demand

TABLE 8

Per Cent of Teachers in the Secondary Schools of the Public School
Systems and the Approximated Numbers for Each Subject *

(Summary of Tables 11 to 36)

SUBJECT	1898 TOTAL 27,298		1908 TOTAL 43,963		1918 TOTAL 98,209		1928 TOTAL 181,580	
	Number	Per Cent	Number	Per Cent	Number	Per Cent	Number	Per Cent
English	3,699	13.55	6,792	15.45	17,157	17.47	33,356	18.37
Social Sciences (Total)	2,577	9.44	4,766	10.84	9,133	9.30	22,189	12.22
Mathematics	3,120	11.43	6,669	15.17	11,461	11.67	19,411	10.69
Commercial	2,858	10.47	3,201	7.28	9,615	9.79	17,468	9.62
Sciences (Total)	4,840	17.73	5,126	11.66	9,870	10.05	14,418	7.94
Trades	1,215	4.45	3,372	7.67	7,984	8.13	14,236	7.84
Modern Languages (Total)	1,884	6.90	4,647	10.57	8,859	9.02	12,692	6.99
History	1,916	7.02	3,794	8.63	7,749	7.89	12,983	7.15
Physical Education	497	1.82	1,042	2.37	3,820	3.89	12,257	6.75
Home Economics	445	1.63	558	1.27	5,863	5.97	9,769	5.38
Art and Drawing	1,460	5.35	2,831	6.44	5,087	5.18	8,059	4.93
French	743	2.72	1,424	3.24	2,495	2.54	6,591	3.63
Music	248	.91	462	1.05	2,259	2.30	5,593	3.08
Latin and Greek	2,825	10.35	3,306	7.52	4,321	4.40	4,957	2.73
Spanish	98	.36	312	.71	1,935	1.97	4,848	2.67
Biology	1,875	6.87	2,110	4.80	1,434	1.46	4,394	2.42
General Science	0	0	88	.20	589	.60	4,086	2.25
Social Studies	0	0	0	0	108	.11	3,160	1.74
Civics	478	1.75	211	.48	511	.52	2,923	1.61
Geography	180	.66	765	1.74	845	.86	2,470	1.36
Chemistry	1,065	3.90	1,046	2.38	1,581	1.61	2,233	1.23
Physics	1,553	5.69	1,024	2.33	1,935	1.97	1,525	.84
Hygiene	341	1.27	207	.47	982	1.00	1,035	.57
German	1,040	3.81	2,981	6.78	4,429	4.51	1,453	.80

*Numbers were obtained from the application of per cents to total number
of public and private secondary schools of the country as given by the *Biennial
Survey of Education, 1924-26.*

in these subjects greater than that shown in Table 10, but it
also indicates that the teaching of these subjects is a less stable
occupation than some of the others. Elsbree's figures do not
show whether this turnover was caused by teachers leaving
educational work, changing to some other branch of educational

work, or merely seeking a higher salary in the same kind of teaching position elsewhere.

In order to obtain further light upon the demand, a study was made of the number of persons who had been placed by the Bureau of Educational Service of Teachers College, Columbia University. The placements in all fields, business as well as the

TABLE 9

APPROXIMATED INCREASE IN SECONDARY SCHOOL TEACHERS IN BOTH PUBLIC AND PRIVATE SCHOOLS IN THE UNITED STATES BY DECADES, 1898 TO 1928

(A Summary of Table 8)

SUBJECT	1898-1908	1908-1918	1918-1928
English	3,093	10,365	16,199
Social Sciences (Total)	2,189	4,367	13,056
Mathematics	3,549	4,792	7,950
Commercial	343	6,414	7,853
Sciences (Total)	286	4,744	4,548
Trades	2,157	4,612	6,252
History	1,878	3,955	5,234
Modern Languages (Total)	2,763	4,212	3,833
Physical Education	545	2,778	8,437
Home Economics	113	5,305	3,906
Art	1,371	2,256	3,865
French	681	1,071	4,096
Music	214	1,797	3,334
Latin	481	1,015	636
Spanish	214	1,623	2,913
Biology	235	676	2,960
General Science	88	501	3,497
Social Studies	0	108	3,052
Civics	267	300	2,412
Geography	585	80	1,625
Chemistry	39	535	652
Physics	529	911	410
Hygiene	134	775	53
German	1,941	1,448	2,976

different branches of education, were obtained by students majoring in the particular subject. The last three columns of Table 10 give the figures for the placements in secondary schools and for the total number of placements.

THE SUPPLY

As a means of finding the relation between supply and demand an investigation was made of the number of persons majoring

TABLE 10

COMPARISON OF SECONDARY SCHOOL DEMANDS WITH SUPPLY *

SUBJECT	PER CENT OF SECONDARY SCHOOL TEACHERS (TABLE 8)	INCREASE IN NUMBER OF TEACHERS (TABLE 9)	STUDENTS, MAJORING IN THE SUBJECT AT TEACHERS COLLEGE IN 1927-28 (GRADUATE STUDENTS ONLY) Per Cent	Number	STUDENTS, MAJORING IN THE SUBJECT AT HUNTER COLLEGE IN 1928-29 Per Cent	Number	TEACHERS COLLEGE PLACEMENTS SECONDARY SCHOOLS Per Cent	Number	TOTAL
English	18.37	16,199	17.48	261	1.83	80	20.72	63	138
Social sciences	12.22	13,056	12.73	190	22.05	965	9.21	28	64
Mathematics	10.69	7,960	9.04	135	17.33	759	16.78	51	63
Commercial	9.62	7,853	1.27	19	—	—	3.29	10	—
Sciences	7.94	4,548	10.65	159	14.14	619	9.54	29	62
Trades	7.84	6,252	2.01	30	—	—	.66	2	16
History	7.15	5,234	9.98	149	18.22	798	—	—	—
Modern Languages	6.99	3,333	7.70	115	26.00	1,139	9.87	30	62
Physical Education	6.75	8,437	8.77	131	—	—	6.91	21	100
Health	—	—	1.21	18	—	—	—	—	—
Home Economics	5.38	3,906	14.80	221	—	—	6.91	21	175
Art and Drawing	4.93	3,865	8.10	121	.30	13	5.59	17	99
French	3.63	4,096	5.56	83	18.13	794	—	—	—
Music	3.08	636	4.82	72	3.17	139	1.31	4	35
Latin and Greek	2.73	2,013	1.41	21	8.29	363	8.22	25	27
Spanish	2.67	2,960	1.01	15	3.90	171	—	—	—
Biology	2.42	3,457	—	—	12.40	543	—	—	—
General Science	2.25	3,652	—	—	—	—	—	—	—
Social Studies	1.74	2,412	—	—	—	—	—	—	—
Civics	1.61	1,625	.54	8	.91	40	—	—	—
Geography	1.36	652	.73	11	—	—	—	—	—
Chemistry	1.23	410	—	—	1.74	76	—	—	—
Physics	.84	33	—	—	—	—	—	—	—
Hygiene	.57	—	1.14	18	.96	42	—	—	—
Geology	.002	—	—	—	—	—	—	—	—
Astronomy	.004	2,976	—	—	—	—	—	—	—
German	.50	—	—	17	3.97	174	—	—	—
Political Science	—	—	—	—	1.44	62	—	—	—
Economics	—	—	—	—	1.48	65	—	—	—
Pre-Medical	—	—	—	—	2.10	92	—	—	—
Physiology	—	—	—	—	3.83	168	—	—	—
Educational Sociology	—	—	1.47	22	—	—	—	—	—

* Comparison is based on data of Tables 8 and 9 and the placements made by the Bureau of Educational Service of Teachers College, Columbia University, as against the number and per cent of students majoring in each subject at Teachers College, and at Hunter College, New York City.

in the several branches of education in teacher-training institutions. Two such institutions were chosen: Teachers College, Columbia University, and Hunter College of the City of New York.

The Dean's Report of Teachers College furnished the information concerning the number of graduate students majoring in the various departments. Corresponding figures for the undergraduate students were not available.

The figures for Hunter College were obtained from the Registrar's records. They give the enrollment by majors and the percentages of the total student body in all four years.

The data for both Teachers College and Hunter College are given in Table 10. This table should be read as follows: Teachers of English comprise, according to this study, 18.37 per cent of the total secondary school teaching staff. The net increase in number of English teachers for the decade 1918-1928 for the country as a whole was approximately 16,199, or about 1,620 additional English teachers yearly, not taking into consideration the turnover. The Teachers College enrollment of graduate students majoring in English for the year 1927-28 was 261, or 17.45 per cent of the graduate enrollment training for secondary school subjects. The Hunter College enrollment of English majors for 1928-29 was 80, or 1.83 per cent of the total enrollment. The Bureau of Educational Service of Teachers College placed 63 English teachers in high school positions— 20.72 per cent of high school placements. It placed a total of 138 persons in different kinds of English positions—a few more than half of those majoring in English.

It is interesting to note how fairly consistent the per cents in the graduate enrollment at Teachers College are with the per cents in secondary education in the field. In only a few places—where it would be expected, as in trades, commercial subjects, and home economics—do they differ very widely. This fact does not imply that Teachers College is filling the need in the field, for different teacher-training institutions specialize along different lines. In Hunter College there seems to be little connection between the demand in the field and the supply offered.

Several factors should be taken into consideration in reading Table 10:

1. The figures for Teachers College were for graduate students who had come from the, field and knew the demand. The students at Hunter College were undergraduates who had less knowledge of the demand. The figures from Hunter College show very definitely the need for vocational guidance of such students.

2. The Teachers College graduate students are preparing for supervisory work and for college and university positions as well as for high school teaching. The figures in the first two columns of Table 10 are for high school teachers only.

3. The figures given by the Bureau of Educational Service of Teachers College—for both total positions and secondary school positions—relate to graduate and undergraduate students, whereas the figures of the Teachers College enrollments by majors relate to graduate students only.

4. Many of the Teachers College graduate students were on leave of absence and so did not desire placement. Many were placed by heads of departments or by commercial agencies, and not by the Bureau of Educational Service.

Another interesting comparison is that of the demand as estimated for 1928 in the second column of Table 10 with the study of supply and demand in teacher training made in Ohio on 1923 figures.[2] The order of importance according to demand of the two studies is given in the lists on page 44.

The present study agrees strikingly with the Ohio study in many respects. It differs in finding a smaller demand for teachers of Latin, physiology, general science, and geology. Some of the causes for these differences may be the following:

1. The Ohio study takes turnover into consideration, whereas this study does not.

2. The Ohio study is based on figures gathered in one state, whereas this study gives figures estimated from a sampling of the country as a whole.

3. The Ohio study is based on figures for 1923; this study for 1928.

4. The Ohio study is based on both rural and urban schools; this is based on urban schools alone.[3]

[2] Buckingham, B. R., *Supply and Demand in Teacher Training*, pp. 95-98.

[3] The Sixth Yearbook, Department of Superintendence, National Education Association (p. 365), makes the following statement concerning the effect of the size of the community on the study of modern languages and Latin : "The

5. The trends in 1928 showed mathematics and Latin going down and trades and physical education and general science going up.

ORDER OF IMPORTANCE OF DEMAND FOR TEACHERS

THIS STUDY	THE OHIO STATE STUDY
English	English
Social sciences (total)	History and civics
Physical education	Mathematics
Mathematics	Home economics
Commercial subjects	General science
Trades	Latin
History	Commercial subjects
French	Physical training
Home economics	Geography
Art and drawing	Music
General science	Manual training
Music	Biology
General social	French
Biology	Agriculture
Spanish	Drawing and art
Civics	Physics
Geography	Physiology
Chemistry	Chemistry
Hygiene	Economics
Physics	Spanish
German	Sociology
	Industrial arts

CONCLUSIONS

The following conclusions may be drawn from these facts:

1. In Teachers College, Columbia University, the per cent of graduate students in secondary education is, in all but a few subjects, almost the same as the per cent of secondary school teachers in the field.

2. In Hunter College, New York City, there seems to be little connection between the supply as represented by the number of students in the several branches of education and the demand in the field.

---

percentage of modern language enrollment varies directly and the percentage of Latin enrollment varies inversely with the size of the community. That is, modern languages are an urban subject, and Latin enrollment is larger in the rural communities."

CHAPTER VII

IMPLICATIONS FOR THE FUTURE OF TRENDS, INFLUENCES, AND DEMAND AND SUPPLY OF EACH SUBJECT OF THE SECONDARY SCHOOL CURRICULUM

ENGLISH

Trends.—English had a steady average increase in number of teachers in secondary schools from 1898 to 1928 in the cities studied. Table 11, however, shows no such trend in percentage. In Baltimore there was an increase between the years 1908 and 1918 but none during the decade 1918-1928. The percentage in Pittsburgh and Warren has vacillated, with the peak at 1918. In Philadelphia there was a steady and substantial increase, probably due in most part to the fact that in 1898 a large number of the schools there were taught in German. As the large German population in Philadelphia became Americanized, less emphasis was placed on German and more on English. The number of teachers of English in Los Angeles decreased from 24 per cent to 15 per cent.

The average percentage of teachers of English in the large cities has increased, but the great variety of increase and decrease in the different cities makes conclusions uncertain. Had other cities been studied it is possible that English might not have shown an increase.

In all the cities studied, however, the per cent of teachers of English was higher than the per cent of teachers in any other subject. At least two causes contributed to this, though there may be others as well: (1) English is a tool subject of demonstrated value for all; and (2) English is required in all secondary schools.

Present Demand and Supply.—At a very conservative estimate an average of 1,619 new teachers of English are added yearly in the high schools of the country; they constitute 18 per cent of the total high school teaching force. With the turnover on the total 16,199 this number would be greatly increased. Buckingham states the demand for Ohio alone to be 1,000 teachers annually.[1] This must mean that Ohio has a very large turnover.

In Teachers College, Columbia University, 17.48 per cent of the graduate students are majoring in English. Of 138 English teachers placed by that institution, 63 were placed in secondary school positions. This number was 20.72 per cent of secondary school placements.

TABLE 11

NUMBER AND PER CENT OF ENGLISH TEACHERS IN THE HIGH SCHOOLS
OF THIRTEEN CITIES

CITY	1898		1908		1918		1928	
	Num-ber	Per Cent	Num-ber	Per Cent	Num-ber	Per Cent	Num-ber	Per Cent
Baltimore	– –	– –	21.17	16.67	45.33	18.69	164.50	18.76
Los Angeles ...	8.00	24.24	27.00	20.61	148.00	17.81	630.50	15.18
Philadelphia ..	22.84	12.52	37.00	12.63	121.50	15.36	454.50	18.08
Pittsburgh	5.50	10.19	11.00	15.49	91.00	20.59	204.34	17.99
Providence	– –	– –	– –	– –	26.00	15.34	57.67	17.87
Warren	1.00	16.67	1.50	15.00	4.00	20.51	7.00	15.38
Boston	– –	– –	– –	– –	– –	– –	285.00	16.88
Buffalo	– –	– –	– –	– –	– –	– –	153.50	19.09
Cleveland	– –	– –	– –	– –	– –	– –	374.00	20.46
Newark	– –	– –	– –	– –	– –	– –	68.00	17.30
New York.....	– –	– –	– –	– –	– –	– –	1,613.00	20.03
St. Louis	– –	– –	– –	– –	– –	– –	163.67	17.83
Waltham	– –	– –	– –	– –	– –	– –	12.94	16.57
Total Number .	37.34	– –	97.67	– –	435.83	– –	4,188.52	– –
Total Per Cent	– –	13.55	– –	15.45	– –	17.47	– –	18.37

Hunter College had only 80 majoring in English, or 1.83 per cent of its entire four-year enrollment. This low number is attributed to the fact that all students are required to take a certain amount of English, but are not allowed to major in it until the junior year.

Prediction.—Very little can be said concerning the future except that the per cent of educators who teach English will probably remain as high as, if not higher than, the number of teachers in any other subject. The better the teaching methods used, probably the greater the numbers who will elect English because

[1] Buckingham, *op. cit.*, p. 96.

of its cultural value. It would seem, therefore, that to teach English in high school is an aim that opens up an ever-widening avenue of usefulness in the future for the young teacher. On the other hand, an important point to be considered is the fact that in many schools a little English teaching in connection with other subjects is required of all teachers. This would lower the demand for specialized teachers of English.

SOCIAL SCIENCES

Trends.—The social sciences have had a varying career. The average of the cities studied started at 9.44 per cent in 1898, rose to 10.84 per cent in 1908, dropped again to 9.30 per cent in 1918 and rose to 12.22 per cent in 1928. There seems to be no uniformity in the different cities studied. In Baltimore and Warren the peak was in 1928; in Providence it was in 1918; in Philadelphia in 1908; in Los Angeles it was in 1898.

The social science group includes teachers of geography, history, civics, and courses called "social studies." The geography, history, and civics courses showed a great variety of per cents with seemingly no pattern. The social studies course was just beginning in 1918 and in some cities had increased to as much as 9 per cent of the secondary school teaching staff in 1928. This trend may be regarded as one phase of the generalizing of subjects for purposes of instruction at the junior high school level. It more than counteracts the decline in some of the separate social studies and probably accounts for it.

Present Demand and Supply.—The social science courses showed a rapid growth in both percentage and total number of teachers. The demand for teachers in 1928 was greater than in any other subject except English. Approximately 1,300 new teachers were added. The turnover of the 22,189 total social science teachers would greatly increase this number.

History teachers constitute the largest group in the social sciences. There is an approximate demand for 523 teachers; the general course comes next, calling for 305 teachers. Civics lost about 26 teachers a year for the decade 1898-1908, but is on the upward trend now. Geography is slowly increasing in total number of teachers though not in percentage.

Teachers College in 1928 had 190 (12.73 per cent) graduate students majoring in the social sciences. The percentage was the same as the percentage of demand in the field. A disproportionate number of these, however, 149 (9.98 per cent), were majoring in history. Teachers College placed 64 teachers in social science positions; 28 of these were in secondary school positions and comprised 9.21 per cent of secondary school placements.

Hunter College had 965 students majoring in social science, 798 of whom were majoring in history. The percentages in

TABLE 12

NUMBER AND PER CENT OF TEACHERS OF SOCIAL SCIENCES IN THE HIGH SCHOOLS OF THE CITIES LISTED

CITY	1898		1908		1918		1928	
	Num-ber	Per Cent	Num-ber	Per Cent	Num-ber	Per Cent	Num-ber	Per Cent
Baltimore	--	--	14.83	11.69	21.17	8.73	130.00	14.82
Los Angeles ...	4.50	13.64	11.17	8.53	80.50	9.68	444.83	10.71
Philadelphia ..	15.50	8.48	34.50	11.78	80.00	10.11	261.00	10.38
Pittsburgh	6.00	11.11	7.00	9.85	28.17	6.37	126.67	11.16
Providence	--	--	--	--	20.17	11.91	30.34	9.40
Warren	--	--	1.00	10.00	2.00	10.26	5.50	13.75
Boston	--	--	--	--	--	--	252.17	14.93
Buffalo	--	--	--	--	--	--	70.00	8.71
Cleveland	--	--	--	--	--	--	242.00	13.24
Newark	--	--	--	--	--	--	50.84	12.94
New York.....	--	--	--	--	--	--	1,021.50	12.68
St. Louis	--	--	--	--	--	--	141.17	15.38
Waltham	--	--	--	--	--	--	10.50	13.54
Total Number.	26.00	--	68.50	--	232.00	--	2,786.52	--
Total Per Cent	--	9.44	--	10.84	--	9.30	--	12.22

both subjects, 22 per cent and 18 per cent, were much higher than the relative demand in the field.

Predictions.—The present emphasis on socializing the curriculum, which is probably in its infancy, seems to indicate that the rise in the percentage of social science teachers between 1918 and 1928, as shown by the average per cents, will continue for the next few years at least. However, those studying the social sciences should prepare for the general work, as none of the percentages, except in the general course, show a rapid increase. Moreover, the data from the two institutions studied show that the supply seems to be exceeding the demand.

TABLE 13
NUMBER AND PER CENT OF HISTORY TEACHERS IN THE HIGH SCHOOLS OF THE CITIES LISTED

CITY	1898		1908		1918		1928	
	Number	Per Cent	Number	Per Cent	Number	Per Cent	Number	Per Cent
Baltimore	--	--	10.17	8.01	15.17	6.26	--	--
Los Angeles ...	2.50	7.58	8.34	6.37	61.67	7.42	155.50	3.74
Philadelphia ..	10.83	5.93	29.00	9.90	75.50	9.54	261.00	10.38
Pittsburgh	6.00	11.11	6.00	8.45	23.50	5.32	66.33	5.84
Providence	--	--	--	--	19.00	11.21	28.67	8.88
Warren	--	--	1.00	10.00	2.00	10.26	5.50	13.75
Boston	--	--	--	--	--	--	153.00	9.06
Buffalo	--	--	--	--	--	--	22.00	2.74
Cleveland	--	--	--	--	--	--	--	--
Newark	--	--	--	--	--	--	30.50	7.76
New York.....	--	--	--	--	--	--	674.00	8.37
St. Louis......	--	--	--	--	--	--	38.00	4.14
Waltham	--	--	--	--	--	--	2.50	3.22
Total Number.	19.33	--	54.51	--	196.84	--	1,437.00	--
Total Per Cent	--	7.02	--	8.63	--	7.89	--	7.15

TABLE 14
NUMBER AND PER CENT OF TEACHERS OF SOCIAL STUDIES IN THE HIGH SCHOOLS OF THE CITIES LISTED

CITY	1898		1908		1918		1928	
	Number	Per Cent	Number	Per Cent	Number	Per Cent	Number	Per Cent
Baltimore	--	--	--	--	--	--	--	--
Los Angeles ...	--	--	--	--	2.00	.24	169.67	4.09
Philadelphia ..	--	--	--	--	--	--	--	--
Pittsburgh	--	--	--	--	.67	.15	37.33	3.29
Providence	--	--	--	--	--	--	5.00	1.55
Warren	--	--	--	--	--	--	--	--
Boston	--	--	--	--	--	--	--	--
Buffalo	--	--	--	--	--	--	47.50	5.91
Cleveland	--	--	--	--	--	--	--	--
Newark	--	--	--	--	--	--	--	--
New York.....	--	--	--	--	--	--	--	--
St. Louis......	--	--	--	--	--	--	83.67	9.11
Waltham	--	--	--	--	--	--	5.50	7.10
Total Number.	--	--	--	--	2.67	--	348.67	--
Total Per Cent	--	--	--	--	--	.11	--	1.74

TABLE 15

NUMBER AND PER CENT OF CIVICS TEACHERS IN THE
HIGH SCHOOLS OF THE CITIES LISTED

CITY	1898		1908		1918		1928	
	Num-ber	Per Cent	Num-ber	Per Cent	Num-ber	Per Cent	Num-ber	Per Cent
Baltimore	--	--	1.50	1.18	6.00	2.47	--	--
Los Angeles ...	2.00	6.06	1.00	.76	5.33	.64	84.83	2.04
Philadelphia ..	2.83	1.55	--	--	.50	.06	--	--
Pittsburgh	--	--	.50	.70	.50	.11	4.50	.40
Providence	--	--	--	--	.67	.40	1.67	.52
Warren	--	--	--	--	--	--	--	--
Boston	--	--	--	--	--	--	22.33	1.32
Buffalo	--	--	--	--	--	--	4.00	.50
Cleveland	--	--	--	--	--	--	--	--
Newark	--	--	--	--	--	--	15.17	3.86
New York.....	--	--	--	--	--	--	180.50	2.24
St. Louis	--	--	--	--	--	--	8.00	.87
Waltham	--	--	--	--	--	--	2.50	3.22
Total Number.	4.83	--	3.00	--	13.00	--	323.50	--
Total Per Cent	--	1.75	--	.48	--	.52	--	1.61

TABLE 16

NUMBER AND PER CENT OF GEOGRAPHY TEACHERS IN THE
HIGH SCHOOLS OF THE CITIES LISTED

CITY	1898		1908		1918		1928	
	Num-ber	Per Cent	Num-ber	Per Cent	Num-ber	Per Cent	Num-ber	Per Cent
Baltimore	--	--	3.17	2.50	2.50	1.03	--	--
Los Angeles ...	--	--	1.83	1.40	11.50	1.38	31.00	.75
Philadelphia ..	1.83	1.00	5.50	1.88	4.00	.51	--	--
Pittsburgh	--	--	.50	.70	3.00	.68	18.50	1.63
Providence	--	--	--	--	.50	.30	--	--
Warren	--	--	--	--	--	--	--	--
Boston	--	--	--	--	--	--	76.84	4.55
Buffalo	--	--	--	--	--	--	.50	.06
Cleveland	--	--	--	--	--	--	--	--
Newark	--	--	--	--	--	--	5.17	1.32
New York.....	--	--	--	--	--	--	167.00	2.07
St. Louis	--	--	--	--	--	--	11.50	1.26
Waltham	--	--	--	--	--	--	--	--
Total Number.	1.83	--	11.00	--	21.50	--	310.50	--
Total Per Cent	--	.66	--	1.74	--	.86	--	1.36

MATHEMATICS

Trends.—In the cities studied mathematics reached its peak in 1908. There was a rapid increase in the number of teachers from 1898 to 1908 and as rapid a decrease from 1918 to 1928. Mathematics now stands third in point of numbers among the secondary school teachers. Not only was there a drop in the average percentage of mathematics teachers but the drop was general in all the cities except Warren. The increase there in 1918 is probably due to the adding of a new mathematics teacher to so small a total as 19.

Most of the sources used did not list algebra, geometry, arithmetic, and general mathematics separately; it is therefore not possible to ascertain the trends in the different subjects. It would be interesting to know if the separate subjects are losing out and if general mathematics is gaining, as was true in the physical and biological sciences and the social sciences.

Contributing Factors.—The following statements present some of the influences which may direct the trends in the teaching of mathematics. The first factor mentioned would tend to maintain or increase the number of teachers. The other factors would tend to decrease the number.

1. College requirements. Mathematics is still required for entrance to most colleges. As long as this continues the number of mathematics teachers will probably not decline very rapidly.

2. The popularization of the secondary school education. This influx into high schools of many children who find it extremely difficult, if not impossible, to learn algebra and geometry has made it necessary to offer courses where these are not required.

3. The tendency to shift the emphasis from cultural and disciplinary training to training which has practical social value. Whereas arithmetic is considered socially and vocationally necessary, the value of the higher forms of mathematics, which were originally given for their disciplinary value, is beginning to be questioned.

Present Demand and Supply.—In 1928 there was need for approximately 795 additional mathematics teachers out of a total of 19,411. The large total indicates a fairly large turnover in addition to the 795 new teachers.

TABLE 17

NUMBER AND PER CENT OF MATHEMATICS TEACHERS IN THE
HIGH SCHOOLS OF THE CITIES LISTED

CITY	1898		1908		1918		1928	
	Num-ber	Per Cent	Num-ber	Per Cent	Num-ber	Per Cent	Num-ber	Per Cent
Baltimore	– –	– –	20.67	16.28	33.33	13.74	102.50	11.69
Los Angeles ...	7.00	21.21	18.17	13.87	81.33	9.79	341.84	8.23
Philadelphia ..	19.50	10.69	47.00	16.04	99.50	12.58	318.00	12.65
Pittsburgh	4.00	7.41	9.00	12.68	51.33	11.61	125.00	11.00
Providence	– –	– –	– –	– –	22.67	13.37	30.67	9.52
Warren	1.00	16.67	1.00	10.00	3.00	15.38	4.00	10.00
Boston	– –	– –	– –	– –	– –	– –	181.67	10.76
Buffalo	– –	– –	– –	– –	– –	– –	100.50	12.50
Cleveland	– –	– –	– –	– –	– –	– –	256.00	14.00
Newark	– –	– –	– –	– –	– –	– –	54.33	13.82
New York.....	– –	– –	– –	– –	– –	– –	830.00	10.30
St. Louis	– –	– –	– –	– –	– –	– –	84.50	9.20
Waltham	– –	– –	– –	– –	– –	– –	9.00	11.61
Total Number .	31.50	– –	95.84	– –	291.16	– –	2,438.00	– –
Total Per Cent	– –	11.43	– –	15.17	– –	11.67	– –	10.69

In Teachers College 135 graduate students (9.04 per cent) majored in mathematics. The Bureau of Educational Service placed 63 teachers, both graduate and undergraduate; this number was less than one-half of the number of graduate students majoring in mathematics. Fifty-one (16.78 per cent) were placed in secondary school positions. In Hunter College 759 students (17.33 per cent) majored in mathematics. If Hunter College is at all a fair sample of undergraduate tendencies, the field will be oversupplied.

Prediction.—Because of its unquestioned value, mathematics will never drop low in point of number of teachers required. When the higher forms are no longer required for college entrance the weeding out of certain kinds of mathematics will go on more rapidly. In all probability mathematics will continue to decline more and more rapidly till a certain minimum, which may not be very low, is reached.

The threatened decline and the oversupply of mathematics teachers makes the field less promising than some others. However, with the present 10.69 per cent of the total secondary teachers teaching mathematics, there is a fair chance of obtaining a good position. It is recommended, however, that the would-be teacher of mathematics prepare to teach general mathematics instead of specializing.

COMMERCIAL COURSES

Trends.—According to the cities studied, the peaks of the commercial courses were in 1898 and 1918. They dropped rather rapidly from 1898 to 1908 and rose almost as rapidly in 1918. The averages for 1918 and 1928 were practically the same. The

TABLE 18

NUMBER AND PER CENT OF COMMERCIAL TEACHERS IN THE
HIGH SCHOOLS OF THE CITIES LISTED

CITY	1898		1908		1918		1928	
	Num-ber	Per Cent	Num-ber	Per Cent	Num-ber	Per Cent	Num-ber	Per Cent
Baltimore	– –	– –	6.00	4.72	18.17	7.49	78.00	8.89
Los Angeles ...	2.50	7.57	12.00	9.17	85.16	10.26	401.67	9.68
Philadelphia ..	12.33	6.75	14.50	4.95	69.50	8.79	200.00	8.00
Pittsburgh	14.00	25.93	12.50	17.61	56.00	12.67	111.66	9.83
Providence	– –	– –	– –	– –	12.50	7.38	41.00	13.32
Warren	– –	– –	1.00	10.00	3.00	15.38	6.00	15.00
Boston	– –	– –	– –	– –	– –	– –	178.50	10.58
Buffalo	– –	– –	– –	– –		– –	49.00	6.09
Cleveland	– –	– –	– –	– –	– –	– –	103.00	5.64
Newark	– –	– –	– –	– –	– – '		36.33	9.25
New York.....	– –	– –	– –	– –	– –	– –	903.00	11.21
St. Louis	– –	– –	– –	– –	– –	– –	44.16	8.41
Waltham	– –	– –	– –	– –	– –	– –	9.00	11.61
Total Number .	28.83	– –	46.00	– –	244.33	– –	2,194.32	– –
Total Per Cent	– –	10.47	– –	7.28	– –	9.79	– –	9.62

individual cities differed widely. Had other cities been studied, it is by no means certain that the curve on Chart 5 would have looked the same. Baltimore showed a constant rise and Pittsburgh a constant decline. Los Angeles, Philadelphia, and Warren reached the peak in 1918; they show only a slight decline from 1918 to 1928.

Present Demand and Supply.—Although the percentage of teachers of commercial subjects has not increased greatly, the demand for new teachers in 1928 was 785. If, in addition, the turnover of the 17,468 then being employed were to be included, this number would be greatly increased.

This study has little record of supply. Teachers College had only 19 (1.27 per cent) of its graduate students majoring in commercial subjects. Ten of these were placed in secondary school positions. This number was 3.29 per cent of secondary school placements. Hunter College does not train for commercial courses.

Predictions.—There is little reason to believe that the percentage of teachers in the commercial courses will change much in the next few years. With the increase in high school population, there will be an increasing demand for commercial courses and for teachers of commercial subjects.

SCIENCES

The sciences include biology, chemistry, physics, and general science courses. Geology and astronomy were of such negligible quantity that they were not included.

Trends.—The percentage of science teachers in 1898 was larger than the percentage of teachers in any other subject, being 17.73 per cent of the total secondary school teaching force. The next highest subject, English, had only 13.55 per cent; and mathematics, 11.43 per cent. The number of science teachers dropped rapidly from 1898 to 1908 and steadily, though more slowly, since then. In each city studied, except Warren, there was a constant drop from 1898. In Warren the highest point was in 1908.

For the separate sciences we find the largest drop in physics. In 1898 physics teachers were 5.69 per cent of the total secondary school force; in 1928 they were only .84 per cent, or less than a sixth of what they had been in 1898. This drop was universal in the cities studied.

In chemistry we find a more gradual decline, from 3.90 per cent in 1898 to 1.23 per cent in 1928. This decline was universal except for Providence where the percentage of teachers of chemistry increased between 1918 and 1928.

The year 1918 showed interest in biology to be at low ebb. Since then there has been a slight increase. Here, again, the different cities varied widely. It is probable that another sampling of cities would yield different findings. In some of the cities studied, data for the separate science courses were not given. Of the four cities for which complete data were obtainable, Philadelphia and Providence showed a decrease, and Los Angeles and Pittsburgh an increase.

The course in general science is rather new in the educational world. In 1898 in the cities studied there was no teacher of such a course. In 1918 Los Angeles was the only city studied which offered it. In 1928 six of the thirteen cities offered it, and 2.25 per cent of the total secondary school teachers were teaching it. The offering of the general course in science is in

TABLE 19
NUMBER AND PER CENT OF SCIENCE TEACHERS IN THE HIGH SCHOOLS OF THE CITIES LISTED

CITY	1898		1908		1918		1928	
	Number	Per Cent	Number	Per Cent	Number	Per Cent	Number	Per Cent
Baltimore	--	--	12.16	9.58	17.83	7.35	43.50	4.96
Los Angeles ...	4.00	12.13	8.00	8.37	55.17	6.64	235.67	5.67
Philadelphia ..	34.84	19.09	41.50	14.16	115.00	14.54	285.00	11.34
Pittsburgh	9.50	17.59	11.00	15.50	39.50	8.94	82.67	7.28
Providence	--	--	--	--	22.17	13.07	33.50	10.37
Warren	.50	8.39	1.00	10.00	1.00	5.13	2.00	5.00
Boston	--	--	--	--	--	--	120.00	7.15
Buffalo	--	--	--	--	--	--	77.00	9.58
Cleveland	--	--	--	--	--	--	155.00	8.48
Newark	--	--	--	--	--	--	28.33	7.21
New York.....	--	--	--	--	--	--	669.00	8.31
St. Louis	--	--	--	--	--	--	71.84	7.82
Waltham	--	--	--	--	--·	--	7.00	9.04
Total Number.	48.84	--	73.66	--	250.67	--	1,811.34	--
Total Per Cent	--	17.73	--	11.16	--	10.05	--	7.94

accordance with the growing practice of offering general courses in certain subjects at the junior high school level. Its rise parallels the decrease in the separate sciences but does not equal it.

Present Demands.—In 1928, 454 additional science teachers were called for out of a total of 14,418. Elsbree found the turnover for science to be the largest of any subject; the number would therefore probably be greatly increased.

In Teachers College 159 graduate students (10.65 per cent) were majoring in the sciences; in Hunter College, 619 (14.14 per cent). The number majoring in science in Hunter College alone exceeded the demand for new teachers of the whole country in 1928. The Bureau of Educational Service of Teachers College

TABLE 20

NUMBER AND PER CENT OF BIOLOGY TEACHERS IN THE
HIGH SCHOOLS OF THE CITIES LISTED

CITY	1898		1908		1918		1928	
	Number	Per Cent	Number	Per Cent	Number	Per Cent	Number	Per Cent
Baltimore	--	--	3.33	2.62	6.00	2.47	--	--
Los Angeles ...	1.50	4.55	3.00	2.29	6.17	.74	45.00	1.08
Philadelphia ..	13.00	7.12	17.00	5.80	17.50	2.21	44.50	1.77
Pittsburgh	4.00	7.41	6.50	9.16	4.00	.90	14.00	1.23
Providence	--	--	--	--	2.50	1.47	3.00	.93
Warren	--	--	--	--	--	--	--	--
Boston	--	--	--	--	--	--	9.50	.56
Buffalo	--	--	--	--	--	--	17.50	2.18
Cleveland	--	--	--	--	--	--	- -	--
Newark	--	--	--	--	--	--	7.17	1.82
New York.....	--	--	--	--	--	--	331.00	4.11
St. Louis	--	--	--	--	--	--	13.00	1.42
Waltham	--	--	--	--	--	--	1.00	1.29
Total Number.	18.50	--	29.83	--	36.17	--	485.67	--
Total Per Cent	--	6.87	--	4.80	--	1.46	--	2.42

TABLE 21

NUMBER AND PER CENT OF GENERAL SCIENCE TEACHERS IN THE
HIGH SCHOOLS OF THE CITIES LISTED

CITY	1898		1908		1918		1928	
	Number	Per Cent	Number	Per Cent	Number	Per Cent	Number	Per Cent
Baltimore	--	--	--	--	--	--	--	--
Los Angeles ...	--	--	1.00	.76	7.00	.84	28.67	.69
Philadelphia ..	--	--	--	--	--	--	159.00	6.33
Pittsburgh	--	--	--	--	4.00	.91	22.00	1.94
Providence	--	--	--	--	2.33	1.38	6.50	2.01
Warren	--	--	--	--	--	--	--	--
Boston	--	--	--	--	--	--	--	--
Buffalo	--	--	--	--	--	--	--	--
Cleveland	--	--	--	--	--	--	--	--
Newark	--	--	--	--	--	--	144.00	1.79
New York.....	--	--	--	--	--	--	25.00	2.72
St. Louis	--	--	--	--	--	--	--	--
Waltham	--	--	--	--	--	--	--	--
Total Number.	--	--	1.00	--	13.33	--	385.17	--
Total Per Cent	--	--	--	.20	--	.60	--	2.25

TABLE 22
NUMBER AND PER CENT OF CHEMISTRY TEACHERS IN THE HIGH SCHOOLS OF THE CITIES LISTED

CITY	1898		1908		1918		1928	
	Number	Per Cent	Number	Per Cent	Number	Per Cent	Number	Per Cent
Baltimore	— —	— —	2.50	1.97	4.00	1.65	— —	— —
Los Angeles ...	1.00	3.03	2.83	2.16	14.84	1.79	47.83	1.15
Philadelphia ..	9.00	4.93	7.50	2.56	13.00	1.64	37.50	1.48
Pittsburgh	.50	.93	2.00	2.82	5.50	1.24	12.50	1.10
Providence	— —	— —	— —	— —	2.50	1.47	6.50	2.01
Warren	— —	— —	— —	— —	— —	— —	— —	— —
Boston	— —	— —	— —	— —	— —	— —	10.33	.61
Buffalo	— —	— —	— —	— —	— —	— —	2.50	.31
Cleveland	— —	— —	— —	— —	— —	— —	— —	— —
Newark	— —	— —	— —	— —	— —	— —	4.17	1.06
New York.....	— —	— —	— —	— —	— —	— —	115.00	1.43
St. Louis	— —	— —	— —	— —	— —	— —	8.00	.87
Waltham	— —	— —	— —	— —	— —	— —	2.00	2.58
Total Number .	10.50	— —	14.83	— —	39.84	— —	246.33	— —
Total Per Cent	— —	3.90	— —	2.38	— —	1.61	— —	1.23

TABLE 23
NUMBER AND PER CENT OF PHYSICS TEACHERS IN THE HIGH SCHOOLS OF THE CITIES LISTED

CITY	1898		1908		＾1918		1928	
	Number	Per Cent	Number	Per Cent	Number	Per Cent	Number	Per Cent
Baltimore	— —	— —	2.00	1.58	6.50	2.68	— —	— —
Los Angeles ...	1.50	4.55	3.00	2.29	14.84	1.79	25.17	.61
Philadelphia ..	11.84	6.49	7.00	2.39	18.00	2.28	32.00	1.27
Pittsburgh	2.00	3.70	2.50	3.52	3.00	.68	4.50	.40
Providence	— —	— —	— —	— —	6.50	3.83	2.17	.67
Warren	— —	— —	— —	— —	— —	— —	— —	— —
Boston	— —	— —	— —	— —	— —	— —	7.83	.46
Buffalo	— —	— —	— —	— —	— —	— —	— —	— —
Cleveland	— —	— —	— —	— —	— —	— —	— —	— —
Newark	— —	— —	— —	— —	— —	— —	7.00	1.78
New York.....	— —	— —	— —	— —	— —	— —	79.00	.98
St. Louis	— —	— —	— —	— —	— —	— —	9.67	1.05
Waltham	— —	— —	— —	— —	— —	— —	.50	.65
Total Number .	15.34	— —	14.50	— —	48.84	— —	167.84	— —
Total Per Cent	— —	5.69	— —	2.33	— —	1.97	— —	.84

TABLE 24

NUMBER AND PER CENT OF GEOLOGY TEACHERS IN THE
HIGH SCHOOLS OF THE CITIES LISTED

CITY	1898		1908		1918		1928	
	Number	Per Cent	Number	Per Cent	Number	Per Cent	Number	Per Cent
Baltimore	--	--	--	--	--	--	--	--
Los Angeles ...	--	--	--	--	--	--	.50	.01
Philadelphia ..	.50	.27	2.00	.68	--	--	--	--
Pittsburgh	.50	.93	.50	.70	--	--	--	--
Providence	--	--	--	--	--	--	--	--
Warren	--	--	--	--	--	--	--	--
Boston	--	--	--	--	--	--	--	--
Buffalo	--	--	--	--	--	--	--	--
Cleveland	--	--	--	--	--	--	--	--
Newark	--	--	--	--	--	--	--	--
New York.....	--	--	--	--	--	--	--	--
St. Louis	--	--	--	--	--	--	--	--
Waltham	--	--	--	--	--	--	--	--
Total Number.	1.00	--	2.50	--	--	--	.50	--
Total Per Cent	--	.36	--	.39	--	--	--	--

TABLE 25

NUMBER AND PER CENT OF ASTRONOMY TEACHERS IN THE
HIGH SCHOOLS OF THE CITIES LISTED

CITY	1898		1908		1918		1928	
	Number	Per Cent	Number	Per Cent	Number	Per Cent	Number	Per Cent
Baltimore	--	--	.33	.26	.50	.21	--	--
Los Angeles ...	--	--	--	--	1.00	.12	--	--
Philadelphia ..	.50	.27	1.00	.34	.50	.06	--	--
Pittsburgh	--	--	--	--	--	--	--	--
Providence	--	--	--	--	.50	.30	--	--
Warren	--	--	--	--	--	--	--	--
Boston	--	--	--	--	--	--	.50	.03
Buffalo	--	--	--	--	--	--	--	--
Cleveland	--	--	--	--	--	--	--	--
Newark	--	--	--	--	--	--	--	--
New York.....	--	--	--	--	--	--	--	--
St. Louis	--	--	--	--	--	--	--	--
Waltham	--	--	--	--	--	--	.50	.65
Total Number.	.50	--	1.33	--	2.50	--	1.00	--
Total Per Cent	--	.18	--	.21	--	.10	--	--

placed a total of 62 science teachers out of 159. Of these 29 (9.54 per cent) were placed in secondary schools. This percentage corresponds fairly well with the percentage of science teachers in service.

Physics showed 410 fewer teachers in 1928 than in 1918, a decrease of 41 each year. Chemistry had only 652 more teachers in 1928 than in 1918. In Hunter College 76 students (1.74 per cent) were majoring in chemistry. This is just about the proportion of teachers in service. Biology showed a decrease of 676 in 1918 over 1908, but the fairly large increase of 2,976 in 1928 more than made this up. There was a small increase also in the percentage. In Hunter College 543 students (12.40 per cent) were majoring in biology. This figure is very much larger than the percentage of teachers in service.

In the general science course there was an annual demand for 349 new teachers. With the very recent start and the growing demand, the turnover would probably be rather small. There is no general science major in college. The Ohio study also found no training for the general courses.[2]

Prediction.—The emphasis on science seemed to reach its height in 1898 or before. Since then the pendulum has been swinging back again, very rapidly at first and more and more slowly since 1908. Probably the rise of the general science course will continue and will partially counteract the decline in the other courses. This would mean that the decline of science will be still more slowed up, and the science curve in Chart 5 will continue to flatten out.

The call for science teachers does not seem to equal the supply. If a student wished to teach science it would be advisable not to specialize, particularly in chemistry and physics. Biology would be little better. The type of science teaching with the surest outlook for the future is the general course.

TRADE COURSES

The name "Trades" as here used includes more than eighty varieties of courses ranging all the way from beauty culture and meat cutting to boat construction. An attempt was made at the beginning of this investigation to separate the industrial arts courses from those taught under the Smith-Hughes Act,

[2] Buckingham, *op. cit.*, p. 97.

because the teachers of the two kinds of courses usually have different training. Since this study is for vocational guidance purposes it was thought best to separate, if possible, the teachers trained in normal schools from those drawn directly from the trades, but as none of the sources made this distinction, the plan was not practicable.

Trends.—The per cent of teachers in the trade courses increased rapidly. The greatest increase in the cities studied was during the decades 1898-1908 and 1918-1928. In the decade

TABLE 26

NUMBER AND PER CENT OF TRADES TEACHERS IN THE
HIGH SCHOOLS OF THE CITIES LISTED

CITY	1898		1908		1918		1928	
	Number	Per Cent	Number	Per Cent	Number	Per Cent	Number	Per Cent
Baltimore	– –	– –	13.00	10.24	23.00	9.48	98.50	11.23
Los Angeles ...	– –	– –	9.00	6.89	73.33	8.82	484.33	11.66
Philadelphia ..	12.00	6.58	26.00	8.87	58.50	7.40	199.00	7.92
Pittsburgh	– –	– –	– –	– –	36.50	8.26	141.50	12.46
Providence	– –	– –	– –	– –	11.00	6.49	34.33	10.64
Warren	.25	4.19	.50	5.00	.50	2.57	3.00	7.50
Boston	– –	– –	– –	– –	– –	– –	149.50	8.86
Buffalo	– –	– –	– –	– –	– –	– –	114.00	14.18
Cleveland	– –	– –	– –	– –	– –	– –	203.00	11.10
Newark	– –	– –	– –	– –	– –	– –	24.00	6.11
St. Louis	– –	– –	– –	– –	– –	– –	60.33	6.57
Waltham	– –	– –	– –	– –	– –	– –	7.00	9.03
Total Number .	12.25	– –	48.50	– –	202.83	– –	1,518.50	– –
Total Per Cent	– –	4.45	– –	7.67	– –	8.13	– –	10.29

1908-1918 there seems to have been no appreciable gain. The tendencies revealed by the average were true also for each individual city studied, all the percentages for 1928 being very much greater than for 1898. In fact, some cities had no industrial arts courses in 1898, and even some had none as late as 1908.[3]

Probable Causes.—Two important tendencies have no doubt accelerated the increase in the number of trade courses offered and consequently the number of teachers.

[3] Numbers for New York City were omitted from 1928 figures because data were not available for the evening high schools.

1. The popularization of secondary school education. This has resulted in the demand that secondary education be practical and in a lowering of the average ability of the high school population.

2. The tendency to shift emphasis from cultural and disciplinary training to training which has practical social value. "Material of greater social use and more directly related to vocation is being emphasized and greater provision for the utilization of pupil activities as a basis for learning is being made."[4] Both of these causes acting on the curriculum and interacting on each other have brought trade courses to the front. On the other hand, inertia and the desire on the part of parents to give their children the same training as they had have prevented a more rapid introduction of trades.

Present Demand and Supply.—There was a yearly demand in 1928 for 625 trade teachers out of a total of 14,236. The turnover on such a large total would make the demand even larger.

Since the supply for trade teachers would scarcely be expected to come from teachers' colleges it is not surprising to find that neither Teachers College nor Hunter College is supplying the demand. In Teachers College, 30 students (2.01 per cent) were majoring in industrial arts and a total of 16 were placed by the Bureau of Educational Service. There is no real measure of supply.

Prediction.—The two causes mentioned above are becoming more and more potent, and the retarding causes are slowly being removed. The upward trend in the number of trade teachers will probably be even more accelerated in the future. The teaching of trades in the secondary schools is a fertile field for the future educator. He should, however, seek other preparation than that furnished by teachers' colleges.

Modern Languages

The writer found French, German, Italian, Spanish, and Esperanto offered for modern languages. Carter V. Good, in a study on the curriculum, adds Norse and Swedish to the list.[5]

Trends.—The peak of modern language study according to the cities studied was in 1908. The percentage of teachers of

[4] *Biennial Survey of Education, 1924-1926*, p. 160.
[5] Good, Carter V., "Titles of Curriculums Offered or Suggested in Secondary Schools," *School Review*, Vol. XXXV, Sept. 1927, pp. 503-9.

modern languages dropped slowly from 1908 to 1918 and then
more rapidly to 1928. Each of the cities studied showed this
decline. It probably would hold good for most other large cities.
Tables 28, 29, and 30 give French, Spanish, and German separately. The peak of German was in 1908. Since then it has
rapidly declined. This drop was shown in all the cities studied,
even Philadelphia with its large German population. The tendency would probably hold true for other large cities.

TABLE 27

NUMBER AND PER CENT OF TEACHERS OF MODERN LANGUAGES IN THE
HIGH SCHOOLS OF THE CITIES LISTED

CITY	1898		1908		1918		1928	
	Num-ber	Per Cent	Num-ber	Per Cent	Num-ber	Per Cent	Num-ber	Per Cent
Baltimore	--	--	15.50	12.20	21.17	8.73	40.00	4.56
Los Angeles ...	3.00	8.34	12.33	9.41	67.67	8.14	207.50	5.00
Philadelphia ..	14.00	7.67	33.50	11.44	94.16	11.91	175.00	6.96
Pittsburgh	1.00	1.85	4.00	5.63	23.50	5.32	37.00	3.26
Providence	--	--	--	--	15.50	9.14	23.83	7.39
Warren	1.00	16.67	1.50	15.00	3.00	15.40	2.50	6.25
Boston	--	--	--	--	--	--	149.00	8.83
Buffalo	--	--	--	--	--	--	48.50	6.04
Cleveland	--	--	--	--	--	--	66.00	3.61
Newark	--	--	--	--	--	--	40.17	10.21
New York.....	--	--	--	--	--	--	764.50	9.49
St. Louis	--	--	--	--	--	--	35.17	3.83
Waltham	--	--	--	--	--	--	4.33	5.60
Total Number .	19.00	--	66.83	--	225.00	--	1,593.50	--
Total Per Cent	--	6.90	--	10.57	--	9.02	--	6.99

French has had its up and downs with no definite trend. The
averages of the cities studied for 1898 and 1918 were almost
the same and the averages for 1908 and 1928 were also almost
the same. The 1908 and 1928 averages were 1 per cent higher
than the 1898 and 1918 averages. There is no noticeable trend
in any of the cities; nor is there a very wide range.

The averages for Spanish showed a constant increase, although
at its peak in 1928 the percentage of Spanish teachers was only
2.67 per cent of all secondary teachers. Except in the case of
Warren, this same increase was shown in all the cities studied.[6]

[6] These same trends were found by Stuart among those preparing to be
teachers. Stuart, Hugh, *The Training of Modern Language Teachers for the
Secondary Schools in the United States*, p. 20.

TABLE 28

NUMBER AND PER CENT OF FRENCH TEACHERS IN THE
HIGH SCHOOLS OF THE CITIES LISTED

CITY	1898		1908		1918		1928	
	Num-ber	Per Cent	Num-ber	Per Cent	Num-ber	Per Cent	Num-ber	Per Cent
Baltimore	--	--	4.50	3.54	5.67	2.34	--	--
Los Angeles ...	1.00	2.78	4.50	3.44	17.16	2.06	41.33	1.00
Philadelphia ..	6.50	3.56	10.50	3.59	30.50	3.86	89.50	3.56
Pittsburgh	--	--	.50	.70	3.00	.68	20.67	1.82
Providence	--	--	--	--	6.50	3.83	11.83	3.67
Warren	--	--	.50	5.00	.50	2.57	1.00	2.50
Boston	--	--	--	--	--	--	96.00	5.69
Buffalo	--	--	--	--	--	--	25.00	3.11
Cleveland	--	--	--	--	--	--	--	--
Newark	--	--	--	--	--	--	12.33	3.14
New York.....	--	--	--	--	--	--	418.00	5.19
St. Louis......	--	--	--	--	--	--	11.17	1.22
Waltham	--	--	--	--	--	--	3.33	4.30
Total Number .	7.50	--	20.50	--	63.33	--	730.16	--
Total Per Cent	--	2.72	--	3.24	--	2.54	--	3.63

TABLE 29

NUMBER AND PER CENT OF SPANISH TEACHERS IN THE
HIGH SCHOOLS OF THE CITIES LISTED

CITY	1898		1908		1918		1928	
	Num-ber	Per Cent	Num-ber	Per Cent	Num-ber	Per Cent	Num-ber	Per Cent
Baltimore	--	--	--	--	1.50	.62	--	--
Los Angeles ...	1.00	2.78	3.50	2.67	34.83	4.19	139.67	3.36
Philadelphia ..	--	--	--	--	7.83	.99	43.00	1.71
Pittsburgh	--	--	--	--	2.50	.57	9.17	.81
Providence	--	--	--	--	1.00	.59	1.00	.31
Warren	--	--	1.00	10.00	1.50	7.70	1.50	3.75
Boston	--	--	--	--	--	--	35.00	2.07
Buffalo	--	--	--	--	--	--	12.00	1.48
Cleveland	--	--	--	--	--	--	--	--
Newark	--	--	--	--	--	--	15.50	3.94
New York.....	--	--	--	--	--	--	264.00	3.28
St. Louis......	--	--	--	--	--	--	16.00	1.74
Waltham	--	--	--	--	--	--	.50	.65
Total Number .	1.00	--	4.50	--	49.15	--	537.34	--
Total Per Cent	--	.36	--	.71	--	1.97	--	2.67

TABLE 30

NUMBER AND PER CENT OF GERMAN TEACHERS IN THE
HIGH SCHOOLS OF THE CITIES LISTED

CITY	1898		1908		1918		1928	
	Num-ber	Per Cent	Num-ber	Per Cent	Num-ber	Per Cent	Num-ber	Per Cent
Baltimore	– –	– –	11.00	8.66	14.00	5.77	– –	– –
Los Angeles ...	1.00	2.78	4.33	3.30	15.67	1.89	8.00	.19
Philadelphia ..	7.50	4.11	23.00	7.85	55.83	7.06	30.50	1.21
Pittsburgh	1.00	1.85	3.50	4.93	18.00	4.07	7.17	.63
Providence	– –	– –	– –	– –	8.00	4.72	2.50	.77
Warren	1.00	16.67	1.00	10.00	1.00	5.13	– –	– –
Boston	– –	– –	– –	– –	– –	– –	16.00	.95
Buffalo	– –	– –	– –	– –	– –	– –	10.50	1.31
Cleveland	– –	– –	– –	– –	– –	– –	– –	– –
Newark	– –	– –	– –	– –	– –	– –	8.50	2.16
New York.....	– –	– –	– –	– –	– –	– –	68.50	.85
St. Louis	– –	– –	– –	– –	– –	– –	8.00	.87
Waltham	– –	– –	– –	– –	– –	– –	.50	.65
Total Number.	10.50	– –	42.83	– –	112.50	– –	160.17	– –
Total Per Cent	– –	3.81	– –	6.78	– –	4.51	– –	.80

Probable Causes.—The drop in the percentage of German
teachers was evidently caused by the war. The rise in the percentage of Spanish teachers was probably a result of the schools'
need for a second language to offer in the place of German, and
also a result of increasing intercourse with South America.

Present Demand and Supply.—Modern languages showed a
rapid drop in percentage but a fairly large total increase in
1928 over 1918. This drop was due to the decrease in German,
French remaining almost the same and Spanish rising.

German showed a decrease in 1928 over 1918 of 2,976 teachers
or 297 per year. In Teachers College 17 graduate students (1.14
per cent) were majoring in German; in Hunter College 147 students (3.97 per cent) were majoring in German. These percentages are both larger than the percentage of teachers in
service. The modern language placements by the Bureau of
Educational Service of Teachers College are listed as a whole,
not separately.

Spanish had a yearly addition of 291. In Teachers College
there were 15 graduate students (1.01 per cent) majoring in
Spanish. This is only a little less than the percentage in the

secondary school field. Hunter College had 171 students (3.90 per cent) majoring in Spanish. This percentage is just a little larger than the percentage of Spanish teachers in service.

The demand for additional French teachers in 1928 was approximately 409. This number should be increased with the turnover of the 6,591 then in service. Teachers College had 83 graduate students (5.78 per cent) majoring in French and Hunter College had 794 students (18.13 per cent). Both of these percentages are higher than the demand, more particularly in the case of Hunter College.

Prediction.—Now that the feeling against Germany is subsiding the study of German will probably slowly regain its place in the curriculum. It is generally conceded that German literature has much in the way of culture and information that is valuable, but withal it is difficult to predict whether German as a language will replace Spanish or whether there will gradually be an increase in modern languages taught in the secondary schools.

If one wished to be a teacher of languages, French would be the safest language to prepare to teach, unless, of course, one could be proficient in several. It would seem unwise at the present time to plan to teach German.

PHYSICAL EDUCATION

"Physical education," as the term is here used, includes dancing, swimming, athletics, military drill, and other activities, but does not include corrective work.

Trends.—In 1898 only one of the four cities where data were gathered had teachers of physical education. In 1928 all of them had. The percentage of these teachers increased rapidly with each decade (see Chart 5). The 1928 percentage varies from 1.24 to 9.08 among the cities. The lower percentage means a later start or a slower growth, but not a decrease. In none of the cities studied was there a decrease at any time.

Probable Causes.—Two developing phases of education have been important factors in the trends in physical education.

1. There is a constantly growing emphasis on physical fitness as in itself part of the good life and also as a foundation for enjoying other things in life.

2. The school is assuming more and more responsibility for

the whole life of the child instead of limiting its scope to intellectual development.

Present Demand and Supply.—The present call for physical education directors is the third largest among high school teachers. There is an annual demand for approximately 843 new directors. Add to this the turnover of the present 12,257 teachers and it will be greatly increased.

Teachers College had 131 graduate students (8.77 per cent) in training in secondary school subjects who majored in physical

TABLE 31

NUMBER AND PER CENT OF TEACHERS OF PHYSICAL EDUCATION IN THE HIGH SCHOOLS OF THE CITIES LISTED

CITY	1898		1908		1918		1928	
	Number	Per Cent	Number	Per Cent	Number	Per Cent	Number	Per Cent
Baltimore	– –	– –	3.00	2.36	7.00	2.89	35.00	3.99
Los Angeles ...	– –	– –	4.00	3.05	37.00	4.45	377.16	9.08
Philadelphia ..	5.00	2.74	8.00	2.73	27.00	3.41	209.00	8.31
Pittsburgh	– –	– –	– –	– –	26.00	5.88	97.00	8.54
Providence	– –	– –	– –	– –	– –	– –	4.00	1.24
Warren	– –	– –	– –	– –	– –	– –	3.00	7.50
Boston	– –	– –	– –	– –	– –	– –	42.00	2.49
Buffalo	– –	– –	– –	– –	– –	– –	26.00	3.23
Cleveland	– –	– –	– –	– –	– –	– –	86.00	4.71
Newark	– –	– –	– –	– –	– –	– –	30.00	7.63
New York.....	– –	– –	– –	– –	– –	– –	581.00	7.21
St. Louis	– –	– –	– –	– –	– –	– –	43.83	4.77
Waltham	– –	– –	– –	– –	– –	– –	5.00	6.45
Total Number.	5.00	– –	15.00	– –	97.00	– –	1,539.00	– –
Total Per Cent	– –	1.82	– –	2.37	– –	3.89	– –	6.75

education. The placement of both physical education and health teachers in secondary schools totaled 21 (6.91 per cent), approximately the same as the percentage in service. The total number of physical education placements was 100, most of them being in universities and colleges and normal schools. Thus the demand seems to be larger in other fields than in the secondary schools.

Prediction.—The combination of the two causes mentioned above has resulted in a constantly growing emphasis on physical education in the schools. There is no present sign of this emphasis changing or decreasing. With the growing high school this would mean an ever-enlarging demand.

HOME ECONOMICS

Home economics does not cover quite so wide a range of subjects as trades. It includes all the sewing, cooking, and homemaking courses. There are as many as 20 of these courses listed.

Trends.—Of the six cities for which data were available in 1908, two cities had no home economics courses. By 1918 all the cities had some teaching along that line. In all cities studied, except Warren, the percentage of teachers in home economics showed a large increase. The average increase was 4 per cent, but during the decade 1918-1928 the increase was smaller. During this period some of the cities increased and some decreased.[7]

Probable Causes.—The same causes which are affecting the trade courses would also cause the upward trend in home economics. The increase, however, seems to have reached its peak and has been slowing down for the past decade. This slowing down is probably caused by two principal factors:

1. The greater number of women earning a living or working as an avocation. The war greatly accelerated this tendency, especially among married women.

2. The mechanization of the home. Stores, bakeries, and delicatessen shops supply the needs of the home and leave the homemaker time for other activities.

Present Demand and Supply.—The present demand for additional home economics teachers is about 390 a year. To this should be added the turnover on the present 9,769 teachers.

Home economics teachers constitute 5.38 per cent of the high school teachers. In 1928 Teachers College had 221 graduate students (14.80 per cent) majoring in that field. It should be remembered, however, that Teachers College emphasizes home economics and probably has a larger percentage than other teachers' colleges. Moreover, the demand in elementary schools and colleges, as well as the demand in business, is as large as, if not larger than, the demand in secondary schools. The Bureau of Educational Service placed 175 home economics

---

[7] The figures for New York City were not included in the home economics data because they did not include the evening and trade high schools, which were included in other cities.

TABLE 32

NUMBER AND PER CENT OF TEACHERS OF HOME ECONOMICS IN THE
HIGH SCHOOLS OF THE CITIES LISTED

CITY	1898		1908		1918		1928	
	Number	Per Cent	Number	Per Cent	Number	Per Cent	Number	Per Cent
Baltimore	– –	– –	2.00	1.58	8.50	3.51	61.00	6.96
Los Angeles ...	– –	– –	5.00	3.82	71.00	8.55	365.67	8.80
Philadelphia ..	4.00	2.20	– –	– –	28.00	3.54	133.00	5.29
Pittsburgh	– –	– –	– –	– –	28.50	6.45	69.66	6.13
Providence	– –	– –	– –	– –	12.00	7.07	23.00	7.13
Warren	.50	8.39	1.00	10.00	1.00	5.13	2.00	5.00
Boston	– –	– –	– –	– –	– –	– –	145.00	8.59
Buffalo	– –	– –	– –	– –	– –	– –	47.50	5.91
Cleveland	– –	– –	– –	– –	– –	– –	115.00	6.29
Newark	– –	– –	– –	– –	– –	– –	12.50	3.18
St. Louis	– –	– –	– –	– –	– –	– –	29.33	3.20
Waltham	– –	– –	– –	– –	– –	– –	5.00	6.45
Total Number.	4.50	– –	8.00	– –	149.00	– –	1,008.66	– –
Total Per Cent	– –	1.63	– –	1.27	– –	5.97	– –	6.90

teachers. Of these, only 21 were placed in secondary school positions or 6.91 per cent of secondary school placements. The demand elsewhere is thus much larger than in secondary schools. Hunter College has no home economics majors.

Prediction.—Whether the causes for increase or the causes for decrease will win out remains to be seen. At the present time, although there is still an increase, it has slowed up. It is impossible to say whether the percentage of teachers in home economics in the secondary schools will continue to increase slowly, will hold its own, or will decrease, in the next decade. However, with the large demand for home economics training in other departments of the school system and in business, it offers opportunities for the future.

ART

Some form of art or drawing has been taught since 1898 in all of the schools studied. In the last few years the variety of subjects grouped under this heading has greatly increased. From the various schools a list of more than 30 varieties of art courses, not including music, was made. The schools varied greatly in the scope of courses offered. Los Angeles offered more than all the others combined.

Trends.—The percentage of art teachers has shown marked variations. The highest point, not only for the average but also for each of the systems studied, was in 1908. Since then there has been a decline. During the last decade the percentage has remained almost constant, and there seems to be no reason for believing that this will change.

There is less variation in the percentage of art and music teachers in all of the systems studied than in any other subjects: for art a little more than 4 per cent, for music a little more than 2 per cent in most of the cities.

TABLE 33

NUMBER AND PER CENT OF ART AND DRAWING TEACHERS IN THE HIGH SCHOOLS OF THE CITIES LISTED

CITY	1898		1908		1918		1928	
	Num-ber	Per Cent	Num-ber	Per Cent	Num-ber	Per Cent	Num-ber	Per Cent
Baltimore	– –	– –	4.33	3.41	8.50	3.51	36.00	4.10
Los Angeles ...	.50	1.51	8.34	6.37	36.67	4.41	186.17	4.48
Philadelphia ..	10.50	5.75	21.00	7.17	52.00	6.57	134.00	5.33
Pittsburgh	3.50	6.48	3.50	4.93	17.50	3.96	45.50	4.01
Providence	– –	– –	– –	– –	14.00	8.26	14.00	4.34
Warren	.25	4.19	.50	5.00	.50	2.57	1.00	3.50
Boston	– –	–	– –	– –	– –	– –	76.17	4.51
Buffalo	– –	– –	– –	– –	– –	– –	30.00	3.73
Cleveland	– –	– –	– –	– –	– –	– –	90.00	4.92
Newark	– –	– –	– –	– –	– –	– –	13.00	3.31
New York.....	– –	– –	– –	– –	– –	– –	456.60	5.67
St. Louis	– –	– –	– –	– –	– –	– –	38.67	4.21
Waltham	– –	– –	– –	– –	– –	– –	3.00	3.87
Total Number.	14.74	– –	40.67	– –	129.17	– –	1,124.11	– –
Total Per Cent	– –	5.35	– –	6.44	– –	5.18	– –	4.93

Present Demand and Supply.—The present demand for additional art teachers is about 386 yearly. The turnover of the 8,952 art teachers now in the schools would increase this number considerably.

There were 121 graduate students (8.10 per cent) studying art in Teachers College in 1928 and 13 students (.30 per cent) in Hunter College. The percentage at Teachers College is almost twice as much as the percentage of teachers in service. The percentage at Hunter College is more than twelve times less than the percentage in service. The Bureau of Educational Service placed 99 art teachers, of whom 17 were placed in secondary schools. This was 5.59 per cent of the secondary school placements.

Prediction.—There is no reason to believe that there will be any less emphasis on drawing in the next ten years than there has been in the past decade. There will probably always be an opening and a future for teachers of art.

MUSIC

Trends.—Music as a subject was listed in four of the five schools studied in 1908. In 1918 Providence was the only city studied that did not have music courses in the high school. The average percentage steadily increased, although the increase was not so rapid as that of the trades, home economics, and the social sciences. Among the individual cities there was both an increase and a decrease in the number of teachers of music. This was probably because the music teacher has always been a special teacher and usually has taught nothing but music. When the number of teachers in a system was small the addition of one teacher who taught nothing but music gave that subject an exaggerated relative importance. These same teachers were sufficient when the total number of teachers had greatly increased. Consequently the percentage waned. For example, Warren in 1898 had a music teacher who gave half of her time to the high school; the ratio to the total staff was 8.39 per cent. In 1908 the city still had one music teacher giving half time to high school, but because the number of teachers had increased the ratio was only 5 per cent of the total, and by 1918, 2.57 per cent.

Present Demand and Supply.—The present demand for music teachers in high schools is approximately 333 per year out of a total of 5,593.

In Teachers College 72 graduate students (4.82 per cent) were majoring in music in 1928. The proportion in service was 3 per cent. The Bureau of Educational Service placed 35 teachers of music. Of these, only 4 were placed in secondary school positions. Hunter College had 139 students (3.17 per cent) majoring in music. This is the same percentage as that of teachers in service.

TABLE 34

NUMBER AND PER CENT OF MUSIC TEACHERS IN THE
HIGH SCHOOLS OF THE CITIES LISTED

CITY	1898		1908		1918		1928	
	Num-ber	Per Cent	Num-ber	Per Cent	Num-ber	Per Cent	Num-ber	Per Cent
Baltimore	– –	– –	.83	.65	.84	.34	15.00	1.71
Los Angeles ...	– –	– –	3.33	2.54	39.00	4.69	202.67	4.88
Philadelphia ..	2.00	1.10	2.00	.68	4.00	.50	71.00	2.82
Pittsburgh	– –	– –	– –	– –	13.00	2.94	47.00	4.17
Providence	– –	– –	– –	– –	– –	– –	8.00	2.48
Warren	.50	8.39	.50	5.00	.50	2.57	1.00	2.50
Boston	– –	– –	– –	– –	– –	– –	42.83	2.54
Buffalo	– –	– –	– –	– –	– –	– –	17.00	2.11
Cleveland	– –	– –	– –	– –	– –	– –	61.00	3.34
Newark	– –	– –	– –	– –	– –	– –	8.00	2.04
New York.....	– –	– –	– –	– –	– –	– –	196.20	2.44
St. Louis	– –	– –	– –	– –	– –	– –	29.00	3.16
Waltham	– –	– –	– –	– –	– –	– –	2.50	3.22
Total Number .	2.50	– –	6.66	– –	57.34	– –	701.20	– –
Total Per Cent	– –	.91	– –	1.05	– –	2.30	– –	3.08

Prediction.—According to the *Sixth Yearbook of the Department of Superintendence of the National Education Association, interest in music is constantly increasing.*[3] The great variety of studies made on all phases of music have shown the wide and varied rôle it has to play in life. This increased appreciation of the place of music in life and the constantly improving methods of teaching it will probably mean that, although music teachers will never comprise a large percentage of the teaching staff, their numbers will increase.

LATIN

Trends.—Chart 5 shows the trend in Latin and Greek for the past thirty years. The number of Greek teachers is so small that these figures are, for practical purposes, representative of Latin teachers. The drop in the percentage of teachers for the twenty-year period 1898-1918 was rapid. From 1918 to 1928 this gradually slowed up, but the percentage is still decreasing more rapidly than that of any other subject. By 1928 the per-

[3] "The Development of the High School Curriculum," *Sixth Yearbook, Department of Superintendence, National Education Association*, pp. 383-96.

centage was only a fourth of what it had been in 1898. This trend was universal, and was marked for each of the cities studied.

TÁBLE 35
NUMBER AND PER CENT OF GREEK AND LATIN TEACHERS IN THE HIGH SCHOOLS OF THE CITIES LISTED

CITY	1898		1908		1918		1928	
	Num- ber	Per Cent	Num- ber	Per Cent	Num- ber	Per Cent	Num- ber	Per Cent
Baltimore	– –	– –	9.67	7.61	17.33	7.15	39.00	4.45
Los Angeles ...	4.50	13.64	9.83	7.50	20.67	2.49	42.83	1.03
Philadelphia ..	15.00	8.22	19.00	6.49	35.33	4.47	71.00	2.82
Pittsburgh	8.00	14.81	8.50	11.97	23.50	5.32	39.00	3.43
Providence	– –	– –	– –	– –	12.00	7.08	12.33	3.82
Warren	1.00	16.67	.50	5.00	1.00	5.13	3.00	7.50
Boston	– –	– –	– –	– –	– –	– –	46.17	2.74
Buffalo	– –	– –	– –	– –	– –	– –	51.00	6.34
Cleveland	– –	– –	– –	– –	– –	– –	38.00	2.08
Newark	– –	– –	– –	– –	– –	– –	24.50	6.23
New York.....	– –	– –	– –	– –	– –	– –	233.50	2.90
St. Louis	– –	– –	– –	– –	– –	– –	20.33	2.22
Waltham	– –	– –	– –	– –	– –	– –	1.83	2.36
Total Number .	28.50	– –	47.50	– –	109.83	– –	622.50	– –
Total Per Cent	– –	10.35	– –	7.52	– –	4.40	– –	2.73

Probable Causes.—The decrease in the number of Latin and Greek teachers, particularly Latin teachers, has been due primarily to the following causes:

1. The great variety of subjects vying for a place in the modern curriculum. The complexity of modern life has made it necessary that subjects be added to the curriculum that were unheard-of two decades ago. The greater number of subjects has meant a smaller percentage for each.

2. The shifting of Latin from a compulsory to an elective subject in most of the public schools. There are three main reasons for this:

a. It is not now required for entrance in most of the colleges.

b. The popularization of secondary school education has resulted in the demand that secondary education be practical. Coincident with this demand has come a lowering of the average ability of the high school population.

c. The emphasis is shifting from cultural and disciplinary training to training which has practical social value. In the *Biennial Survey of Education for 1924-1926* the following statement is made: "A learning science that emphasizes the importance of acquiring habits of adjustment to specific situations rather than an intellectual discipline which is serviceable alike for all, requires for pupils who have varied aptitudes and varied purposes in life, subject matter which is varied in accord with the specific needs of individual pupils." [9] This leaves a place, but not a large place, for Latin in the modern curriculum.

Present Demand and Supply.—The approximate demand for new teachers in 1928 was only 63 for the entire country. This figure will, of course, be increased by the turnover of the present 4,957 teachers.

The figures given in this investigation do not agree with the figures given in the *Classical Investigation of the American Classical League* on the following points:

CLASSICAL INVESTIGATION	THIS INVESTIGATION
"The total enrollment in Latin in the Secondary Schools of the country for the year 1923–1924 is estimated by the United States Bureau of Education at 940,000, slightly in excess of the combined enrollment in all other foreign languages." [10]	In 1918 the number of modern language teachers was twice the number of classical teachers. In 1928 the number of modern language teachers was slightly more than twice the number of classical teachers.
"There are approximately 22,500 teachers of Latin in the Secondary schools of the country." This means more than 12 per cent (1923–24). [11]	In 1918 Latin and Greek teachers comprised 4.4 per cent of all secondary school teachers and in 1928 only 2.73 per cent.

The figures for this investigation are for public schools only, whereas the figures of the Classical Investigation include both private and public schools. The figures of the private schools would have a tendency to raise the percentages.

In the Classical Investigation the statement is made that there is a decreased percentage in Latin enrollment but a total increase. [12] This agrees with the results of the present investigation.

In Teachers College 21 graduate students (1.46 per cent) majored in Latin in 1928. This is an even smaller percentage than is in service in secondary education. However, a total of 27

[9] *Biennial Survey of Education for 1924-1926*, p. 156.
[10] *The Classical Investigation*, Part I, p. 16.
[11] *Ibid.*, p. 17.   [12] *Ibid.*, p. 19.

graduate and undergraduate students of Teachers College were placed in positions.

In Hunter College 363 students (8.29 per cent) were majoring in Latin. If this same percentage should hold true for the other teacher-training colleges, the field will be more than flooded with Latin teachers.

Prediction.—There is no present indication that any of the causes which have resulted in the reduction of Latin will be less active in the near future than they have been in the recent past. In fact, the present trend is to give them more emphasis. This probably means that the Latin curve shown in Chart 5 will continue its downward trend, flattening somewhat as it approaches zero as a limit.

With the percentage of teachers being a fourth of what it was in 1898, the downward trend continuing, and a total of only approximately 63 additional teachers, not including turnover, being called for in 1928, it would seem unwise for a person to plan a career as Latin teacher.

HYGIENE

Hygiene includes corrective physical education, courses in health, home nursing, personal hygiene, wholesome living, and physiology.

Trends.—Of the five school systems for which data were available for the period before 1928, only two had courses in hygiene in 1908. In 1928 there were still five systems of the thirteen cities studied which did not list courses in hygiene. The percentage increased and decreased in the various schools, but there were too few schools with hygiene courses to make the figures of any significance.

It must be remembered that these figures are limited to teachers who engaged only in corrective work and the theoretical phases of health education. During these same years the practical side of health education, carried on by nurses, physicians, and dentists, and by physical education directors, grew enormously.

Present Demand and Supply.—In 1928 hygiene demanded an increase of only 5 teachers a year. The turnover among the present 1,035 teachers of this subject would not be significant.

In Teachers College there were 18 graduate students (1.21

TABLE 36
Number and Per Cent of Teachers of Hygiene in the High Schools of the Cities Listed

CITY	1898		1908		1918		1928	
	Num-ber	Per Cent	Num-ber	Per Cent	Num-ber	Per Cent	Num-ber	Per Cent
Baltimore	--	--	--	--	1.33	.55	--	--
Los Angeles ...	1.00	3.03	--	--	17.67	2.13	51.83	1.25
Philadelphia ..	2.50	1.37	2.00	.68	5.00	.63	2.50	.10
Pittsburgh	--	--	1.00	1.41	--	--	1.00	.09
Providence	--	--	--	--	1.00	.59	.50	.16
Warren	--	--	--	--	--	--	--	--
Boston	--	--	--	--	--	--	14.67	.87
Buffalo	--	--	--	--	--	--	--	--
Cleveland	--	--	--	--	--	--	--	--
Newark	--	--	--	--	--	--	1.67	.43
New York.....	--	--	--	--	--	--	29.50	.37
St. Louis	--	--	--	--	--	--	27.17	2.96
Waltham	--	--	--	--	--	--	--	--
Total Number.	3.50	--	3.00	--	25.00	--	128.84	--
Total Per Cent	--	1.27	--	.47	--	1.00	--	.57

per cent) majoring in health education. The placements are not given separately but are listed with the physical education teachers.

In Hunter College there were 168 students (3.83 per cent) majoring in the old physiology course which has practically gone out of existence in the public schools. Of course this may be the old name used with a new health content.

Predictions.—The present emphasis on participation rather than theory, the rapid increase in number of teachers of physical education, and the growing use of physicians and nurses in the schools would seem to indicate that the percentage of the teachers of hygiene will not greatly increase.

On the other hand, there is just beginning to be an awakening to the necessity for boys and girls to obtain a knowledge of sex hygiene in high school. The *Sixth Yearbook of the Department of Superintendence of the National Education Association* emphasizes this.[13] "There is a rapidly spreading demand for the teaching of sex hygiene. . . . This whole subject is not only one of the newest which we have attempted to put into the school

[13] *The Sixth Yearbook, Department of Superintendence, National Education Association*, p. 475.

program, but it is one of the most important. Largely, we are exploring a new field of education, and progress must be slow and made with extreme caution." This might mean a very gradual increase in the percentage of hygiene teachers. The demand, however, might not come for several years, and would probably be for those with medical training.

The growing demand that the health work of the school be undertaken by physicians, nurses, and physical education directors, together with the small annual increase in number of teachers of hygiene, would indicate that the demand for teachers of hygiene is limited. The person who wishes to engage in hygiene work in the public schools should train to be a nurse, or a physician, or a physical director.

CONCLUSIONS

The following conclusions may be drawn from these data:

1. There has been a rapid increase in all of the general courses.

2. English, trades, and physical education have had a large annual increase in numbers and the percentage is also constantly growing.

3. The social studies, general science, Spanish, home economics, art, and music have had a smaller annual increase in numbers, but a constantly growing percentage.

4. History, mathematics, the commercial subjects, and French have had a large annual increase in numbers but the percentage shows no marked growth.

5. German, physics, hygiene, chemistry, civics, geography, biology, and Latin have had either a small annual increase in numbers or an actual decrease which represented a decreasing percentage.

CHAPTER VIII

CONCLUSIONS AND SUGGESTED PROBLEMS

Summary of Findings

The data obtained from the fourteen cities studied in this investigation yielded the following findings:

1. There are in all between 350 and 400 types of positions in the public schools.

2. After the specific field or subject is chosen there are still many forms of specialization from which one may select. For example, there are 17 different kinds of English being taught, 13 kinds of music, 30 kinds of art, and 30 trades.

3. The elementary school teachers comprise more than half of the educational force. The percentage has declined rapidly during the past thirty years.

4. The percentage of kindergarten teachers does not seem to depend upon the size of the city. It has remained practically the same during the past thirty years.

5. The junior high schools began during the decade 1908 to 1918. They have grown rapidly, though in 1928 there were still some cities in which junior high schools had not yet been introduced.

6. The proportions of high school teachers to elementary school teachers ranged from 1 to 4 to 1 to 1. The percentage has been growing steadily.

7. The percentage of persons in administration does not seem to depend on the size of the city. It has remained practically the same during the past thirty years.

8. In the secondary schools, English, the social sciences, mathematics, and the commercial subjects have the largest number of teachers, with English very much in the lead; thirty years ago science led with a wide margin.

9. Latin and hygiene are among those subjects with the fewest teachers. Astronomy and geology have almost disappeared from the curriculum.

10. The personal service division had already started in 1898, and in 1918 almost all cities had such a service. The percentage is slowly increasing.

11. The professional service division was just beginning in 1908, but is not yet universal. The percentage is slowly increasing.

12. There has been a rapid increase in all the general courses.

13. English, trades, and physical education have had a large annual increase in numbers and the percentage is constantly growing.

14. The social studies, general science, Spanish, home economics, art, and music have had a smaller annual increase in numbers, but the percentage is constantly growing.

15. History, mathematics, the commercial subjects, and French have had a large annual increase in numbers, but the percentage is not growing or is scarcely growing.

16. German, physics, hygiene, chemistry, civics, geography, biology, and Latin have had a small annual increase or an actual decrease in number with a decreasing percentage.

17. The supply of undergraduate students, as shown by Hunter College, does not agree with the demand for teachers. This fact points to the need of guidance for prospective educators. Similar conclusion is reached by the Ohio study.

18. The supply of graduate students, as shown by Teachers College, Columbia University, is, in most respects, close to the demand.

19. There is need of more careful records concerning teachers of various subjects so that future studies on demand and supply, teacher turnover, and other phases may be made for guidance purposes.

PROBLEMS FOR FUTURE STUDY

This study is but one of many investigations that should be made as a foundation for scientific guidance of the prospective educators who need this information for a wise preparation. Following are a few of the problems it suggests:

1. A nation-wide investigation of turnover, probably by sections, such as the Elsbree investigation in New York State and the Buckingham investigation in Ohio. Such an investigation should show, among other things, the relation between turnover

and sex, its causes, and its relation to subject matter. It should reveal whether those who leave a position take the same kind of position elsewhere, enter another kind of educational position, or leave education entirely.

2. A study of teaching combinations, like that made in Ohio, covering the country as a whole. It is important in guidance to know what combinations of subjects are most likely to be required.

3. A study of the supply of teachers in the different subjects as shown by majors and minors in the teachers' colleges of the country. This should be compared with the percentages found in the field. It should be kept up to date for purposes of guidance.

4. A study of the mode of entrance into the different educational positions. Are positions entered from a liberal arts college, a teachers' college, a normal college, directly from the trades, or through promotion within the ranks? Is experience required? Are there certain subjects for which special training is not required, but which anyone may be expected to teach?

CHAPTER IX

PRACTICAL APPLICATIONS

The results of this investigation can be put to practical use by several groups of workers. Following are some of these groups.

PROSPECTIVE EDUCATORS

After having chosen the large occupation of educationist the young person desires to know in what field of education to specialize. Within the large group she will have a choice of from three to four hundred jobs. If she limits herself to high school teaching she will find more than three hundred and fifty different subjects being taught in the high schools of the country. If she then limits herself to the teaching of English, for example, she may find seventeen different English courses being offered in the secondary schools. It is quite unlikely that one person could be proficient in all of them. Many of the other subjects include as great a number of courses. There are thirty different subjects that can be classified under the arts, not including the twelve or thirteen under music. There are thirty different trades now being taught, and the number is increasing every year. Information regarding this diversity of opportunity should be available to the young person just starting out on a career.

In deciding what branch of education to enter, personal interests and preferences should be a large factor. The person making the choice should know the probabilities for the future of that particular branch. For example, a student is very fond of music and wants to know what the prospects are for a music teacher in the public high schools. The charts and conclusions of this investigation will show that whereas music is not demanding so large a number of teachers as some of the other subjects it nevertheless has a promising future.

COUNSELORS

Teacher-Training Schools.—Such material is not only valuable for young people, but it is also necessary for the counselor in

80

teacher-training schools. Without it the counselor's advice is based more or less on guess. With it the counselor knows what choices are open to the student and the probable future in each line.

For example, if a student entering a teachers' college wishes to train to be a teacher of hygiene, the counselor can advise that there seems to be very little call at the present and little prospect for the immediate future for teachers of hygiene. The person who wants a school career in hygiene should either become a physical education director or take a nurse's or physician's training.

Seventh and Ninth Grades.—Counselors in the seventh and ninth grades will want this information in a simplified form along with similar information of other occupations to place before the children just entering and just leaving junior high school.

ADMINISTRATORS

City Systems.—Administrators of city systems will find it interesting as well as instructive to compare their systems with these fourteen systems. If they differ radically they might well analyze their situation, and perhaps modify their practices.

For example, Newark in 1928 had only a fourth as many teachers in high schools as in elementary schools. In 1918 the average percentage of teachers in high schools was greater than this, and by 1928 the average number of teachers in high schools was almost half as many as in the elementary schools. At this same time Los Angeles had more high school than elementary school teachers. Newark might well ask itself why it has fallen so far behind in the development of its high schools.

Small Systems.—Administrators of small systems could consider wherein and why their systems should differ from the large systems. They could then compare figures and see if they do so differ.

Teachers' Colleges.—Administrative officers of teachers' colleges will find these results valuable in checking the emphasis put on the different departments. It will help them to keep the supply more nearly corresponding to the demand.

For example, it was found that in one teachers' college there was very little connection between the demand in the field and the number of students majoring in the different departments.

French and biology, for each of which there is a comparatively small demand, were among the departments having the greatest number of majors. In fact, the number of majors for each of these departments in just this one college was larger than the yearly demand for French and biology teachers in the entire country.

For training schools which give no training for a general science course this study should suggest to the administrators that probably it would be wise to introduce such training. Or if as many as 15 per cent of the students were majoring in Latin, the administrators or counselors would see that it might be wise to direct some of them into other courses where the percentage is smaller than the demand.

HISTORIANS

This study will be of interest to the historian of education. It will show him the mathematical results of the historical trends which he studies. It will show him, from the practical standpoint of the school directories, when new branches were added to the educational program and when others were no longer offered. For example, from the data concerning psychologists it is possible to know when school psychologists were first appointed and the percentage holding positions.

SUMMARY

Thus it will be seen that information concerning the kinds of educational tasks available, their present distribution, and their past trends with the probable implications for the future can be of practical value to the young person choosing a life job, to counselors in both grade schools and teacher-training institutions, to administrators in school systems and teacher-training institutions, and to historians of education.

BIBLIOGRAPHY

BUCKINGHAM, B. R. *Supply and Demand in Teacher Training.* University Studies, Vol. 11, No. 15. Ohio State University, Columbus, Ohio, 1926.

ELSBREE, W. S. *Teacher Turnover in the Cities and Villages of New York State.* Contributions to Education, No. 300. Bureau of Publications, Teachers College, Columbia University, 1928.

GOOD, CARTER V. AND GOOD, RAYMOND E. "Titles of Curriculums Offered or Suggested in Secondary Schools." *School Review,* Vol. XXXV, Sept. 1927, pp. 503–9.

GOOD, CARTER V. "The Variables of the Senior High School Curriculum and the College Entrance Problem." *School Review,* Vol. XXXV, Nov. 1927, pp. 686–91.

Biennial Survey of Education, 1924–1926. United States Bureau of Education, Bulletin, 1928, No. 25. Government Printing Office, Washington, D. C.

Keeping Pace with the Advancing Curriculum. Research Bulletin of the National Education Association, Sept. and Nov. 1925.

"The Development of the High School Curriculum." *Sixth Yearbook, Department of Superintendence, National Education Association,* 1928.